WILLIAM BINGHAM 2nd
A LIFE

WILLIAM BINGHAM 2nd
A LIFE

Stanley Russell Howe

Bethel Historical Society

2017

Published by the Bethel Historical Society, Bethel, Maine

Support for this publication has been provided by The William Bingham Foundation, The Betterment Fund Created by the will of William Bingham 2nd, and The Bingham Trust.

Printed in the United States of America

DEDICATION

This volume is dedicated to the memory of Edith Kimball Howe
(1894-1975), who spent seven years in the service of William
Bingham 2nd at his residence in Bethel, Maine. She also was a
Gould Academy classmate and close friend of Eva M. Bean
(GA Class of 1913), founder of the Bethel Historical Society.
Edith Howe was a charter member of that organization.

Edith K. Howe on the grounds of the Bethel
home of William Bingham 2nd, about 1950

CONTENTS

Preface ix

Acknowledgements xiii

Chapter 1 Antecedents and Early Days 1

Chapter 2 Years in the Wilderness and Discovery of Bethel 27

Chapter 3 Life under "King George" 65

Chapter 4 Life with Dr. Walters 125

Notes 139

Index 185

Illustrations following page 88

Preface

One of my earliest memories is of arriving during the early 1950s in the family car at the paved driveway of a green shingle style cottage—William Bingham 2nd's summer home—located at the south end of Broad Street in Bethel, Maine. My mother, father, and I had come to visit my paternal grandmother, who was soon greeting us warmly in the kitchen of this house where she worked for seven summers (1948-1954). All I recall knowing at this stage of my youth was that we were at "Mr. Bingham's" (as he was reverently referred to by nearly everyone in Bethel), sitting in his kitchen visiting with my grandmother. It was a well-equipped room, and as I looked around I couldn't help noticing how much more impressive this kitchen was than the one in our home.

When we left and were driving back to East Bethel, I asked where "Mr. Bingham" was and was told, "he was upstairs." I don't think I really understood the implication of that remark—that he rarely was seen by anyone then—so I continued to hope I would catch a glimpse of him sometime when my family stopped by to visit my grandmother. But I never did, and after the summer of 1954, he failed to return to this house again, having passed away in Miami, Florida, in February of 1955. The closest I ever came to seeing him was undoubtedly the exciting time my grandmother took me up in his personal elevator (the first one I had ever ridden) to the second floor. When we arrived on the upper floor, I recall asking which room was Mr. Bingham's, and my grandmother simply pointed to his door down the hall from the elevator entrance.

So how did my grandmother come to work for Mr. Bingham? Some of her friends urged her to join them in working as a chambermaid during the winter of 1946-47 in Florida's Ormond Beach Hotel. It happened that this was the same hotel in which Mr. Bingham was spending that season in the Sunshine State. Soon thereafter, he and she became acquainted, and he invited her to become part of his household staff in Bethel, where she remained in his employ during the last seven years of his life.

Many years later, in talking with longtime Bethel resident Pearl Ashby Tibbetts (1885-1982), I learned that William Bingham 2nd was, in her words, a "good friend" of my maternal grandfather and her old friend, Harold Stanley (1878-1970). Will had arrived in Bethel in 1911 seeking help from the remarkable Dr. John George Gehring. Sometime between this period and the early 1920s, Will and my grandfather had undoubtedly met while grandfather was operating his horse-drawn meat cart throughout the streets of Bethel Village. During this time, Will wandered freely around the community and was remembered by several local citizens as having been quite "social"; consequently, it is very likely that he encountered my grandfather Stanley and his cart during one of his daily sojourns. They were close in age, born within a year of each other: my grandfather in November 1878 and Will in July of the following year. By this time, my grandfather was married and would eventually have five children, including my mother, who was born in 1920. Will never married, and the extent of this friendship cannot be assessed. Perhaps my grandfather reminded Will of the woodsman and sailor, Edmund "Ned" Fader, whom he befriended in Nova Scotia and spent a winter with in a Canadian logging camp about 1900.

Of course, all of this is merely speculation, but it assists in understanding my lifelong interest in William Bingham 2nd—a fascination that began in the 1950s and has continued through all the years (since 1974) I have been closely associated with the Bethel Historical Society. This outstanding non-profit organization has greatly benefited from the support of the Bingham foundations and individuals connected with Mr. Bingham, particularly his longtime attorney, Sidney W. Davidson, whom I came to know and correspond with until his death in 1979.

Few concerned with the twentieth century history of Bethel, as well as those with a significant connection to Gould Academy, can escape what I call the "Bingham mystique." The fact that few local people ever saw Will Bingham and that even fewer talked or dealt with him personally caused him to become the focus of special, and often considerable, interest in what was (and remains) a small western Maine town in which he played such a low-key but nonetheless leading role. This intriguing phenomenon has induced me to undertake a biography of William Bingham 2nd with the goal of learning all I can about a unique individual who, for the most part, spent his life helping others while living modestly and shunning human contact from the 1920s until the end of his life.

Acknowledgements

Much credit for this book goes to Laurel Blossom, Will Bingham's grand-niece, who assisted me in 2000 when I made a trip to Cleveland to conduct research. She was enormously helpful in providing introductions to many of her family members and making arrangements for me to view and acquire copies of Bingham material at the Payne Archives and Western Reserve Historical Society. Permission for me to access papers about the Bingham family at the Payne Archives was most graciously granted by Charles Bolton, the grandson of Will Bingham's sister, Frances Payne Bolton. I was also assisted in learning more about the Bingham family by Payne Archives Archivist Christopher Eiben, who is remarkably well-informed regarding several branches of the family. He kindly read the manuscript and offered his opinion. Ann Mace, Mr. Bolton's assistant, was most helpful in many ways, including selecting photographs and providing detailed photo identifications. I am also grateful to the staff of the Western Reserve Historical Society for their willingness to make their significant collection of Bingham-related information available to me.

Elaine Ardia, Archives Assistant at the Bates College Edmund S. Muskie Archives and Special Collections Library in Lewiston, Maine, was very helpful in providing me with information on Will Bingham's funding of Muskie's legal education at Cornell University. She also assisted me in locating information about Bingham's financial generosity toward Bates; at the time of his death in 1955, Will Bingham was Bates' largest donor.

I am also grateful to several people who shared their memories of Will Bingham, including John P. Howe II, M.D., who was a Bethel neighborhood youth in Mr. Bingham's later years, and Dr. Arthur Walter's grandson, Peter McWilliams, who assisted by providing a description of Will Bingham's health during his grandfather's association with the great philanthropist. Rebecca Kendall, as a medical assistant, recalled drawing blood from Will Bingham for review by Dr. Willard Boynton. Dr. George Farnsworth's granddaughter, Susan Dale, was generous in sharing family photos and describing life in the Christmas Cove, Maine, area during the time her grandfather was a leading citizen of that picturesque coastal village. I am also grateful to my cousin, James Haines, who accompanied me to Christmas Cove, reproduced pertinent photographs, and took copious notes.

For their financial support of this biographical project, I want to acknowledge the three foundations bearing Will Bingham's name: The William Bingham Foundation, The Betterment Fund Created by the Will of William Bingham 2nd, and The Bingham Trust. To the trustees of each of these organization, I extend my sincere appreciation for making the research, writing, and publication of this book possible. As already mentioned, I am grateful to the various repositories that furnished me with a wide variety of information (letters, memos, reports, photographs, etc.). These included the Payne Family Archives and the Western Reserve Historical Society in Cleveland; the Tufts University Archives in Medford, Massachusetts; the Muskie Archives at Bates College in Lewiston, Maine; the Bethel Historical Society Research Library; the Oxford County (Maine) Registry of Deeds (Eastern District); and the Oxford County (Maine) Probate Office.

I am indebted to Randall Bennett, Executive Director of the Bethel Historical Society, for overseeing this project and exercising his superb editorial skills to ensure its readability and attractive design. To William Chapman, Librarian/Archivist at Bethel

Historical Society, I extend thanks for his technical assistance in preparing the final draft of this book for publication.

It has been a genuine pleasure to research and write this biography, having spent much of my life hearing about Will Bingham through all kinds of connections and connotations. I trust readers will make discoveries here and will forgive any deficiencies that they may notice.

Stanley R. Howe
Hastings Homestead
Bethel, Maine
April 2017

※ 1 ※

Antecedents and Early Days

O N BOTH THE PATERNAL and maternal sides of his ances-
try, William Bingham 2nd (universally known throughout his life to his family and closest associates as "Will")
belonged to the ninth generation of his lineage to reside in what is
today the United States. Coming to America from England during
the 17th century, many of his Bingham and Payne forebears appear
to have been solid and often substantial citizens who migrated
through the years from Connecticut and Massachusetts to New
York and, finally, to Ohio, where William Bingham 2nd was born
on 21 July 1879.[1] Deacon Thomas Bingham, the first in his paternal
line to live in this country, settled in Norwich, Connecticut, in the
1660s and was a proprietor of that town, later moving to nearby
Windham, and—in an era when it was a common occurrence in
some parts of New England—owned slaves. Thomas Bingham's
son and the youngest of eleven children, Stephen Bingham, a
farmer, grew up in Windham, Connecticut, and lived in Andover,
but later returned to Windham. His son, Dr. Eleazer Bingham, was
a self–trained physician who spent most of his life in Andover, Connecticut. The next in line on Will Bingham's paternal side was Ensign Stephen Bingham, who continued the agrarian family tradition
and served in the American Revolution. Stephen's son, Captain
Cyrus Bingham, spent his lifetime as a citizen of Andover,
Connecticut, working the land and milling grain. Captain Cyrus's
son, William Bingham (1816-1904), was born in Andover and
started life laboring on his father's farm, but, longing for a better
way of earning a living, was caught up in the westward migration

that characterized the American experience in the nineteenth century. At the age of twenty, he departed New England for the Western Reserve and settled in Cleveland, Ohio, where, after some uncertainty, he became a businessman and banker. His hardware and metal trade business grew along with the burgeoning city that he now called home.

The origins of Cleveland extend back to Connecticut's colonial claims to land in the Northwest Territory granted in the seventeenth century.[2] To settle these claims, the federal government bestowed upon the state of Connecticut a tract of land known as the "Western Reserve." Due to reluctance on Connecticut's part to administer these lands, they were promptly sold in the fall of 1795 to a group of investors known as the Connecticut Land Company. This body almost immediately undertook a survey to choose a site for a Reserve capital. However, before this effort could be completed, it became necessary to settle Indian land claims stemming from the 1794 Battle of Fallen Timbers, a clash which brought an end to the struggle between American Indian tribes affiliated with the Western Confederacy and the United States for control of the Northwest Territory—an area bounded on the south by the Ohio River, on the west by the Mississippi and on the northeast by the Great Lakes. With this agreement, the Indians took the western portion of the Reserve and the Connecticut Land Company gained the territory to the east and south.

In the spring of 1796, Moses Cleveland and some forty others ventured to the Reserve to lay out the principal settlement overlooking Lake Erie at the mouth of the Cuyahoga River. Not surprisingly, the plan of the town was heavily influenced by New England and New York models, since that was largely the experience of these men. Settlement remained sluggish for several years, but eventually there were enough people in Cleveland to designate it as a port of entry in 1805 and the county seat in 1809. By 1824, the hamlet had evolved into a canal village, and by the 1840s it had grown into a provincial center of commerce. The original inhabitants had mainly come from the British Isles, Scandinavia, and Germany. As the nineteenth century progressed, commercial ventures proliferated, and southern and eastern European immigrants—including Russian Jews, Poles, Hungarians, Czechs, Croatians, Italians and Greeks—flocked to Cleveland to labor in the city's factories and places of commerce.

It was into this world that the first William Bingham—the grandfather of William Bingham 2nd—arrived and seized commercial opportunities offered by the burgeoning city. Although Bingham showed little or no interest in developing into an aspiring politician, he did serve briefly as a city councilor in the mid-1840s, taking particular interest in the waterworks affecting the city. He also became a trustee of Cleveland's sinking fund in the 1860s. When the Civil War broke out in 1861, he supported the Union cause with distinct fervor, encouraging young men to enlist in the great effort of defending the nation from the secessionist threat. The following year, he assumed a leading role in Cleveland's efforts to raise funds for disabled soldiers and in heading up the Cuyahoga County Military Committee. His attention was focused throughout that conflict on furnishing hospitals and the Sanitary Commission with all necessary supplies for war relief.

Following the Civil War, William Bingham refused all efforts by others to draft him for nomination as a candidate for Mayor of Cleveland. Nevertheless, he did serve as a delegate to the Southern Commercial Convention in Cincinnati in 1870 and was elected to the Ohio Senate in 1873. Refusing to be a presidential elector in 1876, he was, however, appointed by President Ulysses S. Grant to the Board of Indian Commissioners, a post from which he resigned the following year. His professional and business dealings in Cleveland were extensive, but his primary focus was directed toward the Cleveland Rolling Mill, where he played a leading role in its success as a producer of iron and steel.

In 1843, William Bingham married Elizabeth Beardsley in Cleveland, and they eventually had three children. Their middle child, Charles William Bingham, was born on May 22, 1846, in Cleveland and would later become the father of William Bingham 2nd, who was named for his grandfather. From his earliest days, Charles Bingham was a precocious offspring who possessed an academic bent and relished educational challenges. He was seemingly infused with a deep desire to grasp any learning opportunities offered him, and applied himself to his studies with a particular zeal and intensity. He received his early education at Cleveland Academy, followed by time at the New Haven Hopkins Grammar School in 1863, where he prepared for admission to college. He entered Yale in 1864, graduating from that institution four years later. While there, he carried a heavy load of both required and elective courses. Additionally, he mastered several languages, including Latin, French, Greek and German. Despite his studious predilections, Charles Bingham also participated in Yale's athletic and social life. He enjoyed sailing, baseball, and fencing, and also took part in musical and theatrical activities. And he developed a remarkable capacity for making friends. All in all, his record at Yale was an outstanding one.

While Charles Bingham displayed a genial and often friendly temperament, he was unquestionably a man of lofty standards and solid principles. For over forty years, he read a page each of Greek, Latin, French, and German aloud every day. In addition, he possessed a high regard for aesthetics, but his mind also settled upon logical conclusions which allowed him to function very successfully in later life as an astute businessman. Like many men of his era and station in life, he was also adventuresome and disposed toward travel. He visited Civil War battlefields while they were still remarkably "fresh" and, upon graduation from Yale, spent three years in Europe hiking through Switzerland and spending large amounts of time in Germany and France. While staying with a family in Paris, he actually experienced the Franco-Prussian War of 1870 first-hand when he was forced to take cover behind the pillars of the Pantheon as soldiers began firing. Soon after this adventure, he spent time in Germany seeking to improve his language skills by attending the University of Celle, near Hanover. While there, he lived with a family headed by an atheist whose youngest daughter nevertheless repeated the same grace before every meal: "Come Lord Jesus, be our Guest and bless that which Thou hast given us." He continued the tradition by using these same words when his own family dined.

Notwithstanding all his European touring and formal education experience, Charles Bingham did not ignore the practical. Even while at Yale, he wrote his father, "I like to hear about your business and it makes me feel like getting to work myself and leave this good-for-nothing inactive life."[3] This professed interest in the business side of things was even in evidence during his honeymoon in Europe, when he visited iron and steel works in Stockholm, Sweden, and St. Petersburg, Russia.

Returning to the United Sates in the fall of 1870, Charles Bingham resumed his study for an M.A. degree from Yale, which was seemingly granted three years after his baccalaureate degree was awarded in 1871. His early employment activities are not so clear, but his first job was presumably with the Cleveland Iron Company, where his father was president. From that time on, his business interests expanded rapidly. By June 1879, he was associated with the firm of W. Bingham & Company, Wholesale Hardware and Metals. At the same time, he served as Secretary of the Cleveland Oat Meal Company and the Cleveland Rolling Mill Company, a subsidiary of the Cleveland Iron Company. His particular connection to the Wampum Coal & Iron Company in Pennsylvania is uncertain, but he signed letters for them in 1880. In 1881, he assumed the presidency of the Standard Tool Company, a post he held until his death in 1929. Surviving correspondence from 1886 and 1887 points to a great interest in coal, copper, and nickel mines.

In addition to these largely industrial interests, Charles Bingham also engaged in banking operations. For example, in 1883 he served as a director of The Citizens Savings & Loan Association. Later, in 1892, he was among those who organized The Western Reserve National Bank. And in 1920, he was named a director of the newly organized Union Trust Company, a position that, again, he held until his demise.

Above and beyond his personal business affiliations, Charles Bingham also served as the agent for his mother, Elizabeth Beardsley Bingham, renting business properties and acquiring stocks. He was also administrator of the Nathan Perry Payne estate; Payne was his wife's brother, who had passed away without leaving a will. These latter interests became increasingly difficult to manage alone, resulting in the creation of The Perry-Payne Company, with Bingham selected as president of the firm and employees helping to administer the company's affairs.

In politics, Charles Bingham was a Republican, though he was never active politically. Nevertheless, his political beliefs undoubtedly influenced his children, particularly his daughter, Frances, who later served as a Republican congresswoman from the Cleveland area from 1940 to 1969. It's worth noting, in this regard, that Will Bingham's political sympathies also remained with the Republican Party throughout his life.

There is no question that Charles Bingham was an exacting man who demanded much of himself, but he also required high standards of his associates. Intellectual, well-educated, and analytical, he was an observant individual who was much in demand for service on the boards of important cultural institutions such as the Union Club, the Western Reserve Historical Society, the Case Library Association, Lake View Cemetery Association, the Huntington Art and Polytechnic Trust, the Horace Kelly Art Foundation, and the Cleveland Museum of Art—among others. In these organizations, he often served as a trustee and/or an officer.

Foreshadowing his son's later proclivity toward an avoidance of publicity, Charles Bingham's numerous philanthropic endeavors were usually carried out anonymously. One example was the founding of a carpenter shop for boys at Cleveland in February 1885. This venture was soon incorporated as the Cleveland Manual Training School Company, where students were instructed in the use of tools and materials, with emphasis upon mechanics, physics, chemistry, and mechanical drawing. Perhaps Charles Bingham's most significant single contribution during his lifetime was the gift of $500,000 presented to the Case School of Applied Science in his home city for the construction and equipping of a mechanical engineering building. Others added to his gift, and his son, William Bingham 2nd, provided a donation equal to the father's for endowment. Upon completion, the imposing structure was dedicated as "The Charles W. Bingham Mechanical Engineering Building"; the imposing structure continues in use today on the campus of Case Western Reserve University.

As a final point—and in contrast to his serious business interests—Charles Bingham enjoyed participating in theatrical productions and giving lectures on esoteric subjects. His personal library, with its extensive and varied holdings, provided him with many hours of pleasant study and reading. Indeed, his children were encouraged to make extensive use of the books in this room throughout their childhood.

In summing up the life and personality of William Bingham 2nd's father, it can be said that he was an able thinker, a voracious reader, and a writer of distinct ability, with a propensity to succeed in business. He possessed strong cultural inclinations, particularly in music, art, and literature: a dedicated family man, he was a violinist with some acting ability and did occasional sketching as well. He took particular interest in the education of his children and advised them to record details of their activities in journal-form for future reference.

Charles Bingham's wife, whom he married in 1876, was Mary Perry Payne—known to her family and close friends as "Molly"—the daughter of one-time U.S. Senator Henry B. Payne and his wife, the former Mary Skinner Perry. Molly Payne Bingham was born in

Cleveland on July 9, 1854, at the "Stone House," a massive, gabled residence which stood at the corner of Euclid Avenue and North Perry Street until it was demolished in the summer of 1941—long after Molly's death in West Palm Beach, Florida, on January 20, 1898, at the relatively young age of forty-three.

Molly Payne Bingham was educated in Cleveland and at private schools in Europe. Here she was given preparation for a leading role in charity work, in addition to philanthropic causes and social events. Before she embarked for Europe, she was engaged in study with other girls in a home with private tutors at Newburgh, New York.

As the youngest of her siblings, Molly enjoyed numerous indulgences from her doting family, but nonetheless remained unspoiled by all the attention, a quality confirmed by her surviving letters. These missives clearly show that she achieved adulthood without losing her great devotion to family and associates, or her loving attitude to the world in general.

Departing for Europe in October 1868, Molly sailed on the *Deutschland* with Sophia Hawthorne, widow of the famed author, Nathaniel Hawthorne, and her two daughters, Una and Rose, and son, Julian. Molly spent two years abroad, missing her sister, Flora's, wedding to William Collins Whitney, but finding enough time around her studies to visit Switzerland and Italy.

Upon her return to the United States, Molly found her days taken up with visits to her sister, Flora Whitney, in New York, as well as to numerous friends residing elsewhere. Of more immediate concern was the fact that her father, Henry B. Payne, had been elected to the U.S. House of Representatives in 1874, and she was needed to accompany him in Washington, D.C., to serve as his hostess at receptions and other events to take the place of her deceased mother.

Molly returned to Cleveland from Washington in 1876 and, that same year, married Charles Bingham. Eventually, she bore Charles five children, in between working in Cleveland with various religious and cultural organizations, including the First Presbyterian Church, the School of Design (founded by her mother), and several children's organizations—particularly the Mary Payne Bingham Kindergarten, which she established.

Charles Bingham and Mary "Molly" Perry Payne were married in Cleveland by the Rev. Hiram C. Hayden on June 8, 1876, and had their first child, Oliver Perry Bingham, on December 2, 1877. A little over eighteen months later, on July 21, 1879, their second child, William Bingham 2nd, was born. Nearly two years passed before their first daughter, Elizabeth Beardsley Bingham, arrived on September 29, 1881. A second daughter, Frances Payne Bingham, entered the world on March 29, 1885. The last offspring to join the family was Henry ("Harry") Bingham, whose birth occurred on December 9, 1887.

Because of Oliver Bingham's delicate health (he developed endocarditis following a bout with scarlet fever), the family was often separated, with Molly seeking particular climates in the South or West where it was believed her son would recover from his ailments. Her husband, Charles, usually remained in Cleveland to tend to his business interests, but kept in close contact with the family. During periods when Molly was away from Cleveland and Charles thoroughly occupied with work, the remaining Bingham children got used to spending time with their Bingham and Payne grandparents.

Where Charles and Molly Bingham resided during the first seven years of their marriage is uncertain, but by 1883 they had built themselves a stylish mansion at 707 Euclid Avenue (after 1906, it became 2445 Euclid Avenue), which by this time had developed into one of the finest residential streets in the nation.[4] It is also difficult to determine where the Bingham children obtained their early education beyond private tutoring. However, what is evident is that Oliver, Will and Harry spent some of their formative years at the University School, a college preparatory school for boys founded in 1890 on what was then known as Giddings Avenue.[5]

Will attended University School with some interruptions from 1890 until 1896. The purpose of the school, as set out by its founders, was to provide an outstanding educational experience that would qualify boys for admission to an elite college without their having to leave home. This was among the first educational institutions of its type, providing what would become very fashionable in future years: the country day-school model of independent education. The founding principal, Newton Mitchell Anderson (1856-1936), who headed the school during the years Will Bingham attended, was deeply committed to an educational program that combined applied technology and training in manual arts with a classical curriculum to graduate young men for entry into a world increasingly dominated by industry and commerce. This emphasis upon the merger of the practical with the academic undoubtedly would have appealed to Charles Bingham, with his background in business and interest in all things cultural and academic.

Will Bingham's academic transcripts at University School reveal a fairly wide range of grades during the period of his attendance.[6] For example, in his first year he earned an "A" in Arithmetic, but by the third he had received a "D" in that subject. In Algebra, he registered a "B" in his fourth year. He failed Woodworking in the year 1894-95, and had yet received a "B" in Woodcarving the previous year. His grades for the rest of his courses—which included Mechanical Drawing, Free Hand Drawing, U.S. History, Plane Geometry, Greek, Latin, Vocal Music, Violin, Physiography, and Physiology—were primarily "A's" and "B's."

A small number of letters survive from Will's University School days to provide insight into his life during this period. For instance, writing on April 2, 1890, to his grandfather from Hamilton, Bermuda, he mentioned being part of a group that included several family members who were fishing from a row boat.[7] In an undated letter to his sister, Frances, he reported going to a play and also to hear a "violinist perform."[8] In another undated letter, again written to Frances, he remarked, "My horse turned out very well."[9] From this correspondence, it is clear that music was becoming one of Will's passions, and that outdoor activities such as fishing and horseback riding had also grown to be enjoyable pursuits for him. Several years later, in April 1896, in a letter to his brother, Oliver, Will reported that "Papa has gotten me a beautiful 'setter' dog and a simply fine gun."[10] He continued in his elation by calling the canine a "beaut" and describing it as "black and white with several brown patches and is very well trained."[11] His expectations for the dog were high, as he remarked, "I am just aching to try him in the field."[12] Will was even more pleased with his father's gift of a gun of English manufacture called a "Greener."[13] He stated, "I tried it and found it fitted me perfectly justly [sic] exactly as good as if it had been made to order, in fact it couldn't have been better."[14] His enthusiasm went even further: "Well by George, Papa got that gun for me," adding rhetorically, "Isn't that fine?"[15] In summation, he wrote, "I never have seen a gun I liked better or half as well."[16] He followed this comment with a description of his plans to attend a trap shoot on the weekend.

The abovementioned letter of April 1896 also contained a reference by Will to "Harrywold" being "almost finished." This name was applied to the Lake Erie house constructed on the site of a Payne family hunting lodge in the early 1890s by Oliver Hazard Payne for his sister, Molly Payne Bingham.[17] It became an important location for Bingham family life for many years and made it possible—with its Lake Erie breezes—for the Binghams to escape from Cleveland's oppressive summer heat.

It was evidently during this period that Will Bingham's educational "journey" took another turn, as he briefly attended Santa Barbara Collegiate School in California for several months. The school was founded in August 1887 because, as an observer noted, "one of the drawbacks of Santa Barbara as a resort for Eastern people has been the want of a good private academy for boys."[18] The organizers of this School were T. H. McCune, M.A., and W. J. H. Wallace, B.A., both graduates of the Royal University of Ireland.[19] It was divided into three departments: Collegiate, Senior Academic, and Junior Academic.[20] Undoubtedly, Molly Bingham must have selected Santa Barbara as one of the favored spots she hoped might assist her oldest son, Oliver, in regaining his health. Whether or not Oliver also attended this school is uncertain, since there seems to be no record of his enrollment. In addition, little correspondence containing Will's reaction to this particular academic experience has survived.

A December 1891 letter from Santa Barbara provides details of Will's befriending two men of Chinese descent, "Sam" and "Hoy," and riding horses on beaches.[21] Interestingly, many of his letters in this period mention musical events, concert programs, and his violin. In one of his undated missives from Santa Barbara to his father, he pleads, "Please be here for the next concert; it will be in the latter part of April—with a great deal of love, Will Bingham."[22] In another letter addressed to his father, he confided that he was getting "sick and sick and sicker of Santa Barbara and the weather."[23] Continuing in this vein, he wrote, "It's just clouds, rain, or fog all the time."[24] He vowed that "if it wasn't for music," he would "leave tomorrow."[25] Despite these disheartening sentiments, during one of the periods of his attendance—according to a report dated February 26, 1892—his progress was reported as "excellent."[26] In the same document, his conduct was judged "very good" and his preparation rated likewise. His grades in English Grammar (95), English Composition (98), Spelling (100), Writing (100), Geography (97) and Arithmetic (92) were excellent, with sixty being the lowest passing number.[27] This report differed from one issued a month earlier, when Will received a 70 in English Composition and an 80 in writing, with all the other grades in the nineties.[28] His conduct fared better in January, with "excellent" recorded, and his progress improved to an "excellent" in February; in both instances, his "preparation" rating was listed as "very good."[29]

A late December letter to his grandfather revealed that the weather "is awful cold."[30] He reported that he had been "working pretty hard with my music now trying to get in an orchestra that my teacher has."[31] His father was visiting the family in Santa Barbara and had hired—to accompany his children—in Will's words, "a chinaman now called Hoi" whom we "like very much."[32] Will also reported that "we are on horseback a good deal of the time now," even attempting "to learn to pick up something from the ground while on the horse."[33] He wrote that even his father had "ridden Queen, the wildest horse in the livery stable a good many times," noting that "it was fun to see her dance around."[34] In addition, Will listed the four horses his family had rented, two for a year, and that his mother was riding "a good deal with us."[35] Moreover, he observed boys coasting not on snow but on the "smooth streets" of the hills of Santa Barbara.[36] He called attention to all the birds he was observing, including roadrunners and hummingbirds. Also noted in this letter was the presence of rats and the fact that he and Oliver had set traps and caught a large one.[37]

In January 1892, in a letter to his father, Will praised the sunny Santa Barbara weather, advised that he missed a rehearsal due to a "bad cold," and was preparing for a forthcoming concert.[38] He noted that his music teacher, Mr. McCoy, was trying to get the violinists to bow in the same direction and how much easier it was to play his violin with a chin rest.[39] Writing that he and Oliver had caught another rat, he also reported good hunting and of shooting the following: two buffalo, one deer, two rattlesnakes, and one ostrich![40] The letter also revealed that both he and his brother had fallen off their horses, but were not seriously hurt.[41] Will also confessed that he had shot another bird and was about to retrieve it when a shrike grabbed it and flew away.[42] Other news contained in this letter denoted that he and Oliver had new suits, had visited a farm, and that their mother had acquired "lots of seeds, some plants and a few cushions for here."[43]

The March 10, 1892, issue of *The Morning Press,* Santa Barbara, included an article on the Amateur Music Club's concert in which Will Bingham was listed as one of the violinists.[44] Writing his father of the experience, he expressed pleasure in "getting through without having any strings break."[45]

In an undated letter to his eldest brother (Oliver's whereabouts at the time is not stated), Will noted his pleasure in a joint venture they were embarking upon together. "Isn't it great," he wrote, "that we are to own the Florida place together?"[46] "Of course," he continued, "I have always been awfully interested in it all, but having a landed interest makes it kind of different."[47] From there, he departed with questions on land surveys, future plans, and tree plantings.

Writing to his brother from University School in December 1895 upon his return to Cleveland, Will recorded having great fun skating on Rockefeller's pond and enjoying "some fine games."[48] His course in mechanical drawing required "three pieces left to do" before the end of the week.[49] He pronounced dancing school going "great" and commented that "the floors after being fixed over are simply fine."[50] He noted that University School Principal Newton Anderson had arranged for him to join a Sunday School class and that he had recently participated in a "fine shoot," despite some difficulties with his gun.[51]

It remains a mystery why Will Bingham transferred to St. Paul's School in Concord, New Hampshire, in the fall of 1896, arriving there as a "Junior." St. Paul's had been founded forty years earlier in 1856 by a prominent Boston physician, George C. Shattuck, Jr., who envisioned a place close to nature where boys could have easy access to fields, trees and bodies of water within a loving circle of supportive adults.[52] Once Shattuck had established a board of trustees, he transferred his country home, buildings and farmland to this entity.

Subsequently, the Board selected a young clergyman, Henry A. Coit, as the first Rector of the School. Coit shared Shattuck's idealistic outlook and tendency toward experimentation, but added a strong religious element to the school's educational atmosphere with an abundance of ceremonial ritualism. By the 1880s, wealthy families were beginning to send their sons to St. Paul's, not for its idyllic qualities, but for its academic rigor and vibrant Christian standards that encouraged the fulfillment of a successful life. The fact that Concord was some distance from financial centers such as New York or even Boston assisted in the belief that these sons of privilege would develop a deep sense of independence and vitality in this semi-remote New Hampshire setting.

In 1893, Dr. Shattuck, the school's most dedicated benefactor and an individual who was always an inspiration and model trustee, passed away; Dr. Coit died two years later in 1895. The latter was succeeded by his brother, Joseph H. Coit, who, at sixty-four, had been vice-rector and was long associated with the institution. The new rector soon began reforming some of the archaic disciplinary rules and traditions of the school, modernizing the curriculum and teaching standards, and bringing in fresh faces on the faculty. It was into this atmosphere and academic environment at St. Paul's that William Bingham 2nd was sent by his parents. Whether the lure of a rural setting, idealistic founding principles, or the emphasis on a religious tradition were factors in the decision to transfer Will to the New Hampshire institution is unknown, but the young man initially appeared quite content with this change.

From surviving letters to family members, it can be determined that, in Will's first month there, he approved of his living quarters in a substantial building called "The School," built in 1879-80, replacing the original building known as "Old School," which was struck by lighting and destroyed by a fast moving fire in 1878. "The alcoves really are not half bad," he wrote in a letter to his mother soon after arrival.[53] "I think there is plenty of room for everything and anyhow you are here only to sleep," he observed. "The fellows right next to me are pretty decent and I think really I am very well situated," though, he noted, "some of the alcoves are as dark as

Egypt."[54] He continued in his assessment of his circumstances:
"The desks have been assigned [and] I got a first rate one."[55] As to
his table assignment, he wrote "I'm at Mr. Palmer's table with
Morley [a fellow Ohioan from Sandusky near Cleveland]."[56] The
food, he declared, was "very good and very plain," but "never more
than soup, meat and potatoes (sometimes no potato), some
vegetable and some simple pudding."[57]

Will conspicuously voiced little enthusiasm for mandatory
chapel which opened each day, and observed that "they are very
strict about what you wear."[58] Though he wrote to his mother the
following week about having adjusted to the church part of life at
St. Paul's, he confirmed having made up his mind to one thing,"
asserting, "I will never be an Episcopalian. . . . there's too much
cant in it."[59] He continued his general criticism about church,
pointing to "the speed with which they read the service, as if they
were in an awful hurry to get through."[60] This behavior, he affirmed,
"makes me tired," adding as an afterthought "and lots of other
things besides."[61]

Will noted that St. Paul's rising bell was at 7 a.m., breakfast at 8
a.m. followed by chapel at 8:45 a.m. His courses, beginning at 9
a.m., included Latin, Greek, Algebra, English, German, Greek
History, and Bible Study, which, he observed, "is no cinch."[62] He
reported that he was learning the Catechism and assured his parents
that he was "all right in everything, but they follow a different plan
than the U.S. [University School] and offer very different things in
their preliminary examinations."[63] In concluding one letter, he
predicted that "I guess it will be all right."[64] In the same light tone,
he decreed the teachers to be "fine," although he admitted to having
reservations concerning "the Greek teacher" whom, he
acknowledged, "reminds me of Mr. Jenkins [from University
School]."[65] He did not think it would be "worthwhile" to have his
bicycle shipped, and noted that the school did not allow guns on
campus, but observed that "some of the boys have them in spite of
the rules."

In October 1896, Will confessed to his parents that he was "weak" in Greek and blamed at least part of his problem on the choice of textbook and the teaching methods employed. He also divulged that he did not "like the teacher at all," adding that "he is a young fellow" who did not compare to Mr. Mitchell, a teacher at University School. In contrast to his admitted vulnerability in Greek, he cited his mastery of Latin where he had achieved a score of fifty-two out of a possible fifty-four points.[66]

To his brother, Oliver, in the fall of 1896, Will reported playing tennis and taking long walks "all around the neighborhood."[67] "The lessons are hard," he acknowledged, "but all the masters are fine."[68] In observing that teachers at St. Paul's were called "masters," he noted that "the whole idea of the school is English and a great many of the masters are English."[69] Reporting that his violin had arrived in "good shape" and that he would start lessons very soon, he attempted to reassure his parents that adding music training to his course load would still be workable, saying, " I will do my best to keep it up you may be sure."[70] In the same letter, he again pronounced all his teachers "splendid" and "very pleasant outside of class," with the exception of "the Greek teacher."[71]

To his father, in a letter dated 11 October 1896, he wrote, "Marks were read out again last night."[72] He acknowledged "losses" in Greek, Algebra, and English, but that he was "perfect in everything else."[73] He went on to assure his father, stating, "I think the Greek will straighten out all right."[74]

In the same letter, Will reported that he took a violin lesson and "will be taking one every Monday."[75] He also recorded that he would "probably be able to practice about three quarters of an hour each day," adding that the teacher "seemed first rate and I will go on in the same book I was using with Mr. Shydler [presumably a teacher at University School in Cleveland]."[76]

In a letter to his mother written later in the month, Will admitted that his adjustment to St. Paul's had been more difficult than he expected.[77] "It's all work, up in the morning at six, work until ten at night," he complained. "It's been harder for me lately because I haven't felt well,"[78] However, to reassure her, he admitted that the reason for his discomfort was "nothing special," but "the same old things nagging me all the time and taking all the enjoyment out of everything."[79] In the same melancholy vein, he continued, "The fellows in my class seem nice enough, but so far I have made no friends."[80]

Despite the somber tone of some of his letters, Will ranked fourth in his Form with a perfect score in "punctuality, industry and decorum."[81] The Rector, J. H. Coit, wrote, "This report conveys a very good impression of William Bingham's first month of St. Paul's School."[82] Coit continued, "We are all much pleased with everything that we see of him."[83] In summation, the Rector affirmed that Will was "upright, manly, and an excellent student."[84]

In November 1896, Will admitted in a letter to his brother Oliver of being "scared" when another student informed him that the Rector wanted to see him.[85] He was greatly relieved to discover that Mr. Coit only "wanted to ask me to supper that night."[86] He found the time not "half bad."[87] The Rector, noted Will, "was quite jolly and interesting."[88] The visit was not without its downside, though, as Will acknowledged to Oliver, "we spent all the evening there and consequently the next day [I] flunked everything."[89]

Physical activity was becoming part of Will's life at St. Paul's. In the same letter to Oliver quoted above, Will observed that "I have been running hare and hands this week everywhere across country."[90] The first run of four miles, he admitted, "nearly killed me," but he later testified that he was now "broken in" and didn't "mind it."[91] In a letter to his father a few days later, he quoted the St. Paul's Athletic Director, who upheld the benefits of running as "about the best thing one could do."[92]

Also in his previously cited letter to Oliver, Will thanked his older brother for sending him an article he [Oliver] had written, which Will termed "great."[93] In contrast to his earlier observation about having made no friends, Will confided to Oliver that he had "grown to know a good many fellows."[94] He even offered to name a few, noting that several of them were fellow Clevelanders.

To his father in early November 1896, Will pronounced that "things were going very successfully" and that he was "having an awfully good time."[95] His optimism continued with his assessment that "lessons go all right."[96] Moreover, despite stating that his "violin teacher isn't much good," he did give that teacher credit for the gift of "some awfully pretty pieces."[97] Near the end of his letter to Oliver, Will noted, "[I manage] to practice almost every day and enjoy it very much."[98]

In a letter written a few days later to his mother, who was about to depart for Palm Beach, Will mentioned that the mother of his Cleveland friend, Morley Hitchcock, was at St. Paul's and had brought all the home news of that city.[99] A friend of his mother as well, Mrs. Hitchcock invited him to tea that evening along with Morley, to which Will vowed to his mother, "Of course I'm going."[100] He continued by reassuring her that his music was so important to him that he stayed up an extra hour each evening to practice.[101] On the running front, he reported that he was giving that up since he was sick after four or five miles and now three times that number was required.[102] In his own defense, he reminded her that all the boys who had run fourteen or fifteen miles had fainted and ended up in the infirmary.[103]

By mid-November 1896, Will penned his mother to tell her more about his running and also made reference to the commendations from two teachers that he had received for his course work in Latin and mathematics. [104] "It was very kind of them to say so and it did me good for I have been working very hard," he reported.[105] Will continued by complaining about how little time was allowed to eat meals ("just fifteen minutes") and declared "the table manners would make you sick."[106]

By November 1896, Will also was focusing on getting his skates from home and commenting joyfully on the prospects of the forthcoming skating season in a letter to his father.[107] He also mentioned that in his second month at St. Paul's, he still ranked fourth in his Form.[108] He described being stricken with "a violent stomach upset and cold."[109] Fortunately, he found the doctor very much to his liking and expected to be "all right again in a few days."[110] He concluded this letter with a plea for some remedy for his disappearing hair, which he observed was coming "out by the handsfull."[111]

That same month, Will wrote his mother about entering a shooting match, "although I have not seen a gun for two months."[112] He complained about too much walking and vowed when he returned from Christmas vacation that he was going "to bring underwear an inch thick."[113]

In a subsequent letter to Oliver, Will described his participation in a shoot in which there were twenty-five participants from St. Paul's.[114] Apparently, not much interest in this activity was displayed by the other students, and they succeeded in breaking it up. The faculty member managing the event was, in Will's words, "so mad that he called the shoot off and refunded the money to all the fellows who had entered."[115] Moreover, Will pronounced the whole affair as "absolutely the biggest fake I was ever in" and declared that "even if they had shot, the trap was so bad it only threw the pigeons about fifty feet" and there was, in his view, not much skill "required to hit them."[116] He continued his narrative to his brother with comments on the length of the chapel service, and spoke of having dinner with the Rector, where, he confessed, he "never ate so much," including "three or four desserts."[117] He concluded his remarks by citing a juggling act as "pretty fair" and a performance of "The Rivals" as "the most wonderful performance I ever saw."[118]

As his days at St. Paul's turned into weeks, Will continued to maintain a regular correspondence with various members of his family. To his mother in late November 1896, he expressed pleasure in his new lamp, affirming how much it had helped his eyes.[119] He described the weather as "rotten," as there had been many days of rain and snow, and regretted that skating had been limited due to the unfavorable temperatures and precipitation.[120] His biggest concern was the examination in the Catechism, which he admitted he was "more afraid of" than "anything else" at St. Paul's.[121] "They make it the most important thing and have bishops come up from Boston to hold the examination," he anxiously explained.[122]

This letter to his mother was followed by another in early December 1896, where he admitted that he was "counting every minute now and can hardly wait these few more days" before he returned to Cleveland.[123] Adding more emphasis, he confided, "I will be gladder to get home than I have ever been in my life over anything."[124] However, he cautioned, "You musn't expect me to look very wonderful" since "my face is worse than ever and as I have not been very well lately I look rather panned out."[125] He admitted that "these days are very hard until the end of the term," explaining that he had "made one final effort to do something in athletics and failed."[126] He announced that he had "tried out for the crew" and divulged that it was "very hard to see everyone pass you by and leave you behind."[127] Admitting feeling "very bitter over it," he asserted, "You must help me get used to it."[128] Of this wrenching experience, Will wrote that "you may say I talk nonsense and that I can do as well in athletics as anyone else but I am so slight of frame that I can do nothing."[129] Adding a touch of finality to this declaration of failure, he added, "It has been proven so."[130]

Will ended his rather disheartening letter with observations concerning one of his Cleveland friends [Morley Hitchcock] whom he was glad to have at St. Paul's.[131] He found him "quite different" from "the one we know at home," since he "stands at the head of his Form" and "thinks of nothing but his lessons" and "even studies at meals."[132]

Concluding this missive to his mother he declared, "I must tell you what your letters are to me."[133] Without them, he wrote, "I could not have finished the term."[134]

In a December 6, 1896 letter to Oliver, penned just before he departed for Cleveland, Will appeared more upbeat, commenting on the "superb skating' available at the time.[135] The skating was so good, in fact, the Rector declared a "Skating Holiday," which Will proclaimed "out of sight."[136] He confided to his brother that he "had more fun playing hockey than I had since I have been up here."[137]

By December 20, 1896, Will was back in Cleveland and writing Oliver about how good it was to be home.[138] He noted that "it seemed like paradise to have some space to move around and a bed that is not a board."[139] He made reference to visiting University School for closing exercises and found it "good sport seeing all the fellows" and spending "the great part of the day there."[140] He and his friend, Morley Hitchcock, toured the new addition with Principal Newton Anderson and pronounced that it added "tremendously to the school."[141] Will concluded this letter by telling Oliver that he and his sister, Betty, went to dancing school with "about the same gang there with some few from the old house."[142]

At the end of the year, Will again wrote Oliver in an upbeat mood. "You have no idea how gay we have been this vacation," he reported, and went on to relate all the dancing parties he had attended "almost every evening."[143] He also reported that his photographic endeavors were progressing well. Later in the letter, he recounted how he and another fellow had gone on a long walk to Cleveland's Wade Park and back, trying to find a moose that had been reported in that vicinity.[144] He expressed his disappointment that the snow and ice had melted, thus putting an end to any rabbit hunting that he had been anticipating.

In early January of 1897, Will proclaimed in a letter to his father that "the gayety [sic] of the vacation is finally over."[145] He went on to describe the last party he had attended and informed his father that the vacation had been "awfully good" and that he and his friends "have been awfully gay."[146] He reported that he had not done any shooting due to the inclement weather.

The following week, upon his return to St. Paul's, Will penned his mother that he "felt quite the old boy coming back" and had stayed busy with "lots of unpacking and seeing all the boys," an experience that he "enjoyed immensely."[147] All of the buoyancy he earlier expressed in his letter was tempered somewhat by the news that he had "managed to get the grip" and was in the infirmary.[148] Nonetheless, even that experience had a positive outcome: "I really haven't had a half bad time," he declared. "Everybody has been mighty nice and I've really had a really good time reading."[149] Explaining that he would probably be able to attend classes the next day, he advised his mother not to "waste any pity on me."[150]

By March of 1897, Will had traveled to West Palm Beach, Florida, on a break from St. Paul's. Here, he wrote his father in Cleveland that he "had some duck shooting that beat anything I ever saw before."[151] After getting the skiff anchored and covered with branches, he "got down as far as [he] could" and waited.[152] For two hours the ducks came, and he started shooting. "My gun got hot," he reported, and "it was awfully exciting, just load, fire, load, fire."[153] When the flight ended, he estimated he had "shot over eighty times" and "had some duck too but I guess I won't say how many."[154]

Despite numerous indications early in 1897 that things were going well for Will, a definite break in his correspondence to the family soon occurred. At long last, a letter dated June 1 arrived in Cleveland which provided evidence that he was then facing some kind of personal crisis. Obviously distraught, Will wrote his father that he had just seen Dr. Shattuck and "had a long talk with him."[155] Reporting abstrusely that "the outcome is rather severe," he nevertheless declared that, despite that verdict, "I feel better about things."[156]

The Dr. Shattuck referred to in the above letter was Frederick Cheever Shattuck (1847-1929), a prominent Boston physician who was the son of George Cheyne Shattuck (1813-1893) and Anne Brune Shattuck.[157] His brother, George Brune Shattuck, was also a member of the first class to graduate from St. Paul's. Frederick Shattuck was later educated at Boston Latin School, Harvard

College, and Harvard Medical School. After training experiences in hospitals in London, Paris and Vienna, he returned to Boston to begin his practice in 1875. Besides his medical pursuits, he also spent considerable time researching and writing history. As a physician, Shattuck was more interested in teaching and research than treating patients, but at the height of his career dealing largely with private patients, Shattuck was, according to one account, "the most noted physician in Boston."[158] For many years, he served as a trustee of St. Paul's, and it was while he was in this capacity that Will Bingham consulted him in the spring of 1897.

Continuing on in his letter to his father, Will declared that Dr. Shattuck had firmly told him that he must "give up work for the present."[159] Will had questioned the necessity of such a drastic move, but Dr. Shattuck assured him with such certainty that he chose not to question further. The Doctor also advised Will to return to Cleveland. "[I was] not in any hurry especially, but when in the course of a few days I was ready."[160] Will's reaction to Shattuck's advice was that it would mean "the loss of one year or perhaps more."[161] Upon reflection, Will concluded that it "would not be so terrible."[162] Ruminating on the near future, he added, "It would not pay to go to college in the condition I'm now in" since "I would get no good out of it."[163]

Will was apparently relieved by Dr. Shattuck's advice, since it allowed him to "let other things go and establish my health which could be accomplished all right."[164] He expressed pleasure with Dr. Shattuck's demeanor, conveying to his father that "he talked as if he were my 'Dutch' Uncle very kindly and straight forward."[165]

From this discussion of Dr. Shattuck's judgements, Will moved on to reassure his parents that they should "not feel badly about this."[166] He predicted that "it's merely a few years and after that I will be strong, and much better able to help you a little than if I go on and do myself up for good now."[167] Branding it "a temporary disappointment," he forecast that he could withstand whatever came "without so much difficulty."[168]

"I fully understand how much you and Mother have to bear," he wrote his father, "but please don't let this add to your burden." With an accepting attitude, Will followed this sentence by proclaiming, "It is my pack, and I claim it."[169] He went on to his parents, saying "[You] have done everything and you are always doing everything for me, and giving me every advantage."[170] That situation made it, he contended, "very hard not helping instead of being a care to you."[171] Nevertheless, he assured them that "before so very many years I will be able to do something and then I will show you in deed how I have appreciated it all."[172] And if that did not sound convincing, Will added ominously, "Some day your son will be a help to you" or, he vowed, will "kick the bucket."[173]

Returning to Cleveland, Will must have pondered deeply on his current situation and, especially, on his future. Two letters composed in the fall of 1898 provide additional insights into his relationships with those around him and, undoubtedly, to what must have been a trying time in his life. Agnes Judson, a sister of the Bingham family tutor, Arthur Judson, wrote to Will, "I am afraid you are the hopeless one, for you do swear so atrociously."[174] In addition, she went on to accuse him in the same letter of poaching game, noting "how bold and bad of you to brave the law as you are doing."[175] Though no rejoinder from Will to these accusations exists or has survived, Miss Judson's letters do suggest that all was not well in the Bingham household—at least as far as Will's behavior was concerned.

Writing to his son around this same time, Charles Bingham attempted to reassure Will by saying he would "see Dr. Shattuck and talk over matters and will not forget to mention malaria."[176] He continued to sound a reassuring tone, telling his son that he felt "confident he [Shattuck] will find something beneficial and interesting."[177] At the same time, Charles Bingham expressed his concern over Will's physical and mental state, saying that he remained "afraid" that Will "would be lonesome during October."[178] His remedy for this perceived condition was to suggest "a couple weeks at the Ottawa Shooting Club," since he also denoted it was possible he might "run over to Chateauguay [Quebec] for a day or so."[179] Once again, there is no surviving evidence to indicate that Will visited the Ottawa Shooting Club. Such was the state of things as Will Bingham embarked on what was to be a lengthy mission of self-discovery.

※ 2 ※

Years in the Wilderness
and Discovery of Bethel

ROM ST. PAUL'S SCHOOL IN NEW HAMPSHIRE, Will Bingham had abruptly returned to Cleveland, and thus ended his formal education and any ambition of attending college. His comings and goings between the time of his departure from St. Paul's in 1897 and his arrival at Dr. Gehring's Bethel Clinic in 1911 are not well documented, and the sources that have survived are indeed fragmentary. To confuse matters further, certain elements of the relevant information appear contradictory.

Various sources provide indications of Will wandering restlessly around the United States and Canada, and, in the latter instance, spending a winter in a Nova Scotia logging camp where he entertained the woodsmen with his violin. This venture occurred about 1900, as recalled by Will in a 1935 handwritten note to his longtime associate, Dr. George Farnsworth, Mrs. Gehring's son by a previous marriage. According to Will, he was befriended that winter by a Nova Scotia sailor and logger named Edmund Fader, whom he called "Ned" and "who acted as a friend and companion to me when I stayed for some time in Chester [Nova Scotia].[180] One can only imagine how challenging, and yet stimulating, this experience must have been for a young man raised among some of America's wealthiest families on Cleveland's elegant Euclid Avenue. Logging camps of this era were not known for their comfort, and the men often slept in one large room of a drafty, crudely erected log structure, on evergreen boughs covered with blankets. Bathing during the winter was quite an undertaking, so it could be infrequent or limited, and it was not unusual for woodsmen to wear the same clothes for weeks or months without a change.[181]

Other of Will Bingham's reported activities during the years immediately after leaving school included horseback riding in Jackson Hole, Wyoming, and several winters spent at resorts in Florida and in Santa Barbara, California. His companion in several of these pursuits was reportedly a young doctor, whose identity remains unknown.[182]

As a young bachelor seeking a variety of experiences with other male companions, Will's life course at this time contrasted with the widespread movement of unmarried men from rural and small towns to large cities.[183] Will's life began in Cleveland and, following his stint at St. Paul's, he traveled to the great outdoors in many parts of North America. As previously mentioned, he met "Ned" Fader during the latter's bachelor days, and spent some time with him in Nova Scotia. Ned later married, had children, and today has many descendants. Other males traveled with him, but they remain unidentified. For several years during his later life, Will employed two bachelor nurses (Guy Bates and James Costello) on his household staff, plus other, female, nurses to provide the twenty-four hour coverage he believed was so essential to his piece of mind and well-being.

A significant source of information for this period of Will's life are the recollections of his sister, Frances Bingham Bolton, who was the family member closest to him throughout his life. She could also relate to him perhaps better than anyone else in the Bingham household because she, too, had spent time at Dr. John G. Gehring's Bethel Clinic during the World War I era (ca. 1914), and developed a lifelong respect and admiration for the famed Doctor and his wife, Marian. As an example of Will's close relationship to his sister, Frances recalled in 1963 a winter memory of Main Street in Bethel when her brother, ". . . took a lot of snow and rubbed my nose in it."[184] She remembered being "furious" with his behavior (and subsequent laughter) at the time, but looked back fondly on the occasion many years later.[185]

From his earliest days, Will appeared to be withdrawn and reserved in a household that was full of activity, and one that could claim prominent family ties to U.S. presidents and cabinet ministers. By most accounts, Will could be characterized as a frail, sensitive, somewhat delicate and reclusive individual, preferring to stay inside reading, playing his violin, and generally avoiding the rougher games and activities of other boys his age. He did, however, occasionally go hunting, swimming, skating, and boating. Because Will restricted his physical activities to avoid contact sports, and appeared prone (especially in later life) to a variety of maladies, his family very likely considered him predisposed to hypochondria, which became more pronounced as he grew older. Furthermore, Robert T. Barr, the son of one of Will's personal advisors in later years, cites remarks made by Frances Bingham Bolton, Will's sister, to Dr. Jean Curran, long a consultant for the Bingham Program, that her brother "had no interest in girls in high school," that his attitude toward life was "puritanical," and that "he was critical of some of the free and easy ways of his companions at the University School in Cleveland."[186] Perhaps affecting his overall sense of well-being, it was around this time that Will reportedly contracted typhoid fever and was seriously ill for an extended period.[187]

A circumstance that undoubtedly affected Will profoundly was the death of his much beloved mother on January 20, 1898, in Palm Beach, Florida, and, just over two years later, the passing of his adored older brother, Oliver, on February 14, 1900, also in West Palm Beach. Will's sister, Frances, recalled at this time that he "found it exceedingly difficult to adjust to the loneliness" that followed these deaths.[188] The passing of his mother and brother were major losses that could not have come at a worse time, with Will facing an uncertain future and the challenge of finding a place in a world in which so many of his forebears and immediate family had so ably succeeded.[189]

For one prone to, as author Francis Parkman noted in *The Gould Academy Story*, "an inherently lonely nature" that brought on extended periods of nervous exhaustion, Will Bingham faced a life marked by anxiety and depression. For a time in this period, he took refuge in staying home and playing his violin. In an effort to pull him out of his depressed state, his father, siblings and various cousins encouraged him to become involved in the family hardware interests, but, as his sister, Frances Bolton, noted, he had no aptitude for or interest in business.

Mrs. Bolton also related that their father Charles, after a harried day at the office, returned home to find Will contentedly playing his violin in the music room of the family's Euclid Avenue residence. Viewing his son as a dilettante, while everyone else in the family took an active role in numerous business and social engagements, Charles reportedly grabbed the violin and, based on this account, "smashed it across the corner of the piano."[190] According to Robert T. Barr, this instance of fatherly disapproval "was the final blow to Will's equanimity, and never again did the two enjoy a father-son relationship."[191] Notwithstanding this statement, later correspondence between Charles and Will in fact reveals a concerned and often protective father providing financial and fatherly advice to his complicated and extremely sensitive son.

Regardless of whether the incident of the shattered violin occurred precisely as some recalled, it appears that Will soon thereafter departed Cleveland, with its associated painful memories, in an attempt to find his niche in the world. The fact was that the inheritance from his mother and the substantial funds settled upon him by other relatives, including his mother's brother, Oliver Hazard Payne (1839-1917), eliminated any concern about finances, thus allowing him to wander the globe freely to determine his life's course. His sister, Frances, wrote that he went out west for a year, and that he "loved" that experience because "it was horses, it was up in the mountains, [and] it was going to many places of beauty and distances."[192] He did return to Cleveland for brief visits every so often, but it was not until he learned that the Gehring Clinic in Bethel, Maine, held a good reputation for helping those with nervous disorders, that his life began to make sense and take a positive turn. It was most likely someone with a Cleveland connection who made Will aware of Bethel, possibly because the celebrated Doctor John George Gehring was born in Cleveland in 1857 and had spent much of his early life there.[193]

Will Bingham's arrival in Bethel in 1911—accompanied by his Cleveland friend, William J. Upson (1878-1936)—brought hope to this complicated thirty-two year old man who had spent a good part of his life, so far, searching for his place in the world. At the time Will entered the Clinic, Dr. Gehring was fifty-four years old. In October of 1888, Gehring had married Marian True Farnsworth, the daughter of Dr. Nathaniel Tuckerman True (1812-1887), a prominent citizen of Bethel, who in 1835 had been the founding principal of Bethel High School. True did not stay on the following year, when the school was officially incorporated as Bethel Academy. Six years later, the struggling Academy, with the promise of a major gift, changed its name to Gould's Academy in honor of the Rev. Daniel Gould, the town's first settled Congregational minister. A Harvard College graduate and soldier of the Revolution, Rev. Gould was living in nearby Rumford at the time of his passing in 1842. Dr. True became principal of the Academy in 1848 and led it with distinction until he was dismissed by the trustees for failing to maintain enough discipline to keep the school from experiencing "wanton vandalism."[194] This connection between the local Academy and the family of Dr. Gehring's wife would soon become a major focus of Will Bingham's life.

Born on the Fourth of July in 1857 of German immigrant parents, John George Gehring was the second of four children. His father operated a grocery store and eventually acquired real estate in Cleveland. Although the family was not wealthy, Gehring was able to attend Western Reserve University, earning his M.D. in 1885. He was later involved with other physicians in the founding of the Cleveland Clinic and was on the medical faculty of the University of Wooster, Ohio, perhaps as a consultant, according to historian William Andrews.[195]

Gehring's departure from Cleveland to the Southwest in the mid-1880s seems to have been precipitated by some kind of nervous exhaustion which led him to seek relief in another setting with a milder climate. While there, he befriended a couple from New England—George and Marian True Farnsworth (the latter of whom was twenty-two years younger than her husband)—an unplanned, but, as will soon become evident, fortuitous meeting. Evidently, there soon developed a close bond, as Dr. Gehring returned with the couple to Boston, where George Bourne Farnsworth, a wealthy retired engineer and Civil War veteran, subsequently passed away in April of 1887. Eighteen months later, in October 1888, John George Gehring married the recently widowed Mrs. Farnsworth, who was seven years his senior.[196]

Following their marriage, the Gehrings visited Europe, spending time in Germany, Italy, and the United Kingdom.[197] During this period, John G. Gehring acquired a Doctor of Science degree in 1891 from the University of Berlin. William Andrews also notes that he is widely believed to have consulted with a Dr. Frederick H. Gerrish (1845-1920) of Portland, who specialized in hypnosis as a treatment for nervous disorders. Andrews also speculates that Gerrish was likely the one who advised Gehring to continue his studies in Europe, since hypnosis was in vogue there.[198] However, because of Marian True Gehring's ties with the State of Maine, it is likely that she urged her husband to seek a medical license to practice in the Pine Tree State. Her remarkable father, Dr. N. T. True, had died the same year (1887) as her first husband and bequeathed to her his homestead built in 1855 at the south end of Bethel's Broad Street; at the time Dr. Gehring received his Maine medical license in 1895, he and his wife were living in her late father's house. Unfortunately, the former residence of N. T. True caught fire in February 1896 and was virtually destroyed while the

Gehrings were away in Portland.[199] A replacement house, possessing distinctive Colonial Revival and Queen Anne features and designed by the Portland, Maine, architect Frederick A. Tompson, was soon erected near the site of the Dr. True house at a cost of approximately $8,000 (about $200,000 in today's money).[200]

It was this new, spacious residence that became the location of Dr. Gehring's Clinic and was to be associated with his work treating patients in his own home. Among his first patients, according to William Andrews, was the Harvard academic Samuel Williston, whose wife had heard good things about Gehring's success with the use of hypnotism to assist the Bay State ornithologist William Brewster in relieving his psychological anxieties.[201]

Physically, John George Gehring was slight in stature, bearded, and bespectacled. Inclined to dress well and formally, he also enjoyed gardening, kept poultry, and took a strong interest in the plantings and landscaping of the grounds surrounding his home. Consistently involved in the Bethel community, Gehring served on a variety of boards including those of both local banks and, most importantly for future implications, that of Gould's (later Gould) Academy. In the latter case, he was selected as vice president in 1905, eventually rising to become the presiding officer of the school's board in 1921. In addition, he was awarded honorary degrees by Bates College in 1923 and Rollins College in Winter Park, Florida, where he may have been influenced by Will Bingham to spend some of his winters with his wife.

During the nearly thirty years of the Clinic's operation, Gehring treated hundreds of persons wealthy enough to afford his care, although he did take on an occasional case without requiring a fee. A good example of this charity was his treatment of the essayist Max Eastman, who spent several weeks in 1906 with Gehring, whom he claimed saved him from "a life of invalidism."[202]

Gehring's techniques involved hypnosis, suggestion and autosuggestion, dietary supervision, regulated periods of rest and exercise, prescribed drugs, and measured socialization. He focused on careful physical treatment of the digestive process as well as other sources of distress from which nervous disorders and troubles can often emanate. In addition, he analyzed his patient's habits, melancholic moods, obsessions, morbid sensations, and other examples of unhealthy mental functions as well as beginnings of breakdowns and all kinds of perceived variations from what could be considered the norm.[203]

Gehring's use of hypnotism was controversial among local Bethel people, as evidenced by the following unidentified observer's account written in 1966 about an incident that occurred in 1912, the year after Will Bingham arrived at the southern end of Broad Street:

> Dr. Gehring, when first married to the widow Farnsworth (nee Susie Marion True), was in limited financial circumstances. He was not accepted as a physician by the people of the Bethel area, hence had no income from local sources. At one time, to earn small change he raised poultry. He waited. The Gehring image was not enhanced by the fact that he was known as a friend and follower of "outlandish" persuasions advocated by the late brilliant and charming Dr. Frederick Gerrish of Portland. Both men had spent considerable time abroad looking into the therapeutic use and value of hypnosis in treatment of mental disease. That was one process far beyond the pale of understanding and acceptance among local citizenry. Gerrish and Gehring were quacks, several degrees below "queer," in the native minds.
>
> In the day when Odeon Hall [on Main Street] was the "Broadway" of Bethel, a traveling hypnotist came to town. To climax his show, he called for a volunteer who would be willing to be put to sleep before the audience. There was considerable derisive whispering—few people really considered such a thing could be accomplished. Finally, one loud-mouthed heckler mounted to the stage—he was beyond the clutches of any witless magic, or so he claimed. He was put under deep hypnosis with no trouble whatsoever—and wound up in the show

window of Elmer Young's harness shop, across the street, where
he lay comfortably resting for all to see until the following day.

Ever afterward, Dr. Gehring was no longer regarded with
scorn. It took an unknown journeyman in the show business to
dispel the down-east disbelief in hypnosis. Henceforward whatever tools the doctor might employ in mental therapy, he
"belonged" in Bethel. Patients came. His fame spread to far
places. He was never accepted with friendly warmth by the
ingrained, doubtful natives of the town, but they agreed that Dr.
Gehring had remarkable success in helping "some mighty queer
people," and a very few sought his help in smoothing snags in
their own personalities. His presence here contributed in no
small way to added employment and a financial boost in Bethel
business.[204]

Usually Gehring began his treatment following a physical examination by requesting that his patients record their individual and
family history. Using this information as a basis to commence his
discussions with some knowledge of both the physical and mental
state of things, he would lay out a plan for making changes in their
behavior and mental attitude. This idealized "partnership" of the
mind and body in healthy communication with each other was an
essential goal of his therapeutic techniques, celebrated in his book,
The Hope of the Variant.

In addition to all the medical, psychological, and dietary advice
and treatment provided by Gehring, his "guests" were encouraged
to dress in their best clothes at regular formal dinners presided over
by the Doctor and his wife, Marian Gehring. There were also
costume parties, musical events, lantern slide presentations, and
lectures offered periodically to the clientele.

"Guests" came from many parts of the nation and often found
the Clinic by word of mouth. Harvard's faculty was so well represented there that, for a time, Bethel's Broad Street was referred to
as the "resting place for Harvard University." Later clients came
from New York and other metropolitan areas in the United States.

Among some of the more noted personalities were George Ellery Hale (1868-1938), a founder of the California Institute of Technology and the Mount Wilson Observatory in Pasadena, California; Franklin K. Lane (1864-1921), who headed the Interstate Commerce Commission during Theodore Roosevelt's administration and served as Secretary of the Interior in President Woodrow Wilson's Cabinet; and Charles A. Culberson (1855-1925), a Texas Governor and U.S. Senator.[205] In addition, one former patient, Robert Herrick (1868-1938), produced a novel, *The Master of the Inn,* which was dedicated to "J.G.G." and featured a character undoubtedly based on Gehring who assists his guests through life's struggles with a variety of procedures, medications, and activities.

Some patients such as George Ellery Hale wrote letters that have survived and offer insights into the daily operations and protocols of the Gehring Clinic. Probably no missive was as "glowing" about Bethel and the Doctor, however, as one written by Franklin K. Lane to Mrs. George Ehle in October 1920 while he was in Dr. Gehring's care:

> Let me tell you Lady Ehle, about this place. It is Nirvana-in-the-Wilderness, the Sacred, Serene Spot. Beautiful, for it is surrounded by mountains—or "mountings"—of gold and green, russet and silver. Noiseless, no dogs bark or cats mew or autos honk. Peaceful—no business. Nothing offends. Isn't that Nirvana? No poverty. People independent, but polite. Children smile back when you talk to them, and you do. And the sky has clouds of color and that casts shadows on purpling mountains and stretches of meadows. Gehring presides, unofficially, modestly, gently; he has given it purpose for being, for here, he does good by healing, and some of his wealthy patients have put up a handsome inn in his honor—and they have said so in a bronze tablet over the mantel. [206]

Lane noted in the same letter that he was cooperating in any way he could with Dr. Gehring, and that the Doctor was trying "ever so hard to touch my trouble-centre, and I shall give him a full chance yet awhile."[207]

At the height of Gehring's fame and influence, former patients organized a group to honor the Doctor and his wife; they called this new organization the "Bethel League."[208] As the first notice recorded, the purpose of the fellowship was to "give an opportunity to its members to return to Bethel once every year, at a given time, for the purpose of renewing the peculiarly warm and sincere friendship which exists between Dr. Gehring and his patients, and also among many of the patients themselves."[209]

The first officers of the Bethel League were Lula W. Sherman of Flushing, New York, as president; Maude Lawrence of Dover Bay, Ohio, as vice president; Will Bingham's business partner, William J. Upson, as secretary; and Bingham himself as treasurer. Annual dues were set at $1. February 12, 1915, was selected as the date for the first reunion, since Bethel, according to the invitation, "presents at this time of year: i.e. skating, tobogganing, skiing, etc. and also because of the wonderful exhilarating quality of the air—a fact which contributes an especial benefit to even a short vacation spent among the beautiful snowclad hills of Bethel."[210]

This reunion was open to all those "who have spent any time at all at Bethel under Dr. Gehring's skillful care." Also welcomed were "all those who have 'learned their lesson' so well that there is no need to return there as patients, who might be glad of an excuse to go back for the pleasure of old friendships, many of which have proved to be the very best and warmest of their lives, chief among them, of course, that of Dr. Gehring himself."[211]

From sources included in the "Bethel League Album" and in the local newspaper, one can gain a number of insights into certain details of the reunion of February 1915. More than twenty attended this first reunion, which largely focused on the banquet held at the newly completed Bethel Inn on February 12. The decorations were elaborate, with the dining room banked with evergreens and hung with American flags. The tables, shaped in the form of a heart and covered with crimson cloth—suggesting the approach of Valentine's Day—underscored the esteem in which the Gehrings were held by those in attendance. The electric lights were encased in red tissue paper to create a soft, rosy glow to the room and contribute to "cozy warmth and geniality."[212] The evergreen boughs reminded those present of "the proximity to the glorious Maine forest."[213] On one of the tables was a modest evergreen tree decorated with small valentines.

The menu for the evening—a copy of which is carefully preserved in the Album—included grapefruit cocktail, essence of chicken, olives, celery, boiled Maine salmon hollandaise, potatoes duchess, broiled sweetbreads with fresh mushrooms, roast native chicken with jelly, mashed potatoes, baked squash, lettuce and tomato salad, vanilla ice cream, assorted cakes and coffee.[214]

After dinner, League president Sherman presented a silver loving cup to the Gehrings, which was inscribed as follows: "Presented to Dr. & Mrs. John George Gehring by Members of the Family as an Expression of Gratitude and Affection, February 12, 1915." Dr. Gehring responded to the gift presentation with what League Secretary Upson described as "a touching and charming speech." A toast of hot milk, reminiscent of their experience as patients, was made to the Gehrings "as a gentle reminder of 'cure' days."[215]

The next day was taken up with a tobogganing party, followed by an evening dance at the Bethel Inn that featured the "Portland Fancy." A staple of the New England dance tradition, the Portland Fancy, often performed to a tune of the same name, regularly appeared on dance cards from the last quarter of the nineteenth century onwards.

On the final day, a snowshoe party was organized with an opportunity for walks and sleighing as the chief diversion, followed by a church service in the evening. The weather proved ideal, although cold, and "all agreed that it was good to be alive, well and back in the 'Homestead' town again under delightful circumstances."[216]

During the Bethel League business meeting, Mary Faulke of Richmond, Indiana, succeeded Mrs. Sherman as President, and Maude Lawrence of Dover Bay, Ohio, the office of Vice President. Both William J. Upson and William Bingham 2nd retained their respective offices.

On September 17-20, 1915, the second meeting of the Bethel League occurred, beginning with a tea at the bungalow on nearby Songo Pond, followed by a dance at the Bethel Inn. The next evening featured the banquet at the Bethel Inn, with the tables decorated with larkspur and shirley poppies. According to the published account, candelabra at each end were formed from birch trees, which reminded those attending of their "former sawing and chopping days"—just one example of the vigorous exercise Dr. Gehring commonly prescribed during his patients' sojourn at the Clinic.[217] The loving cup, presented to the Gehrings the previous February, was also prominently displayed. Dinner offered fruit cocktail, clear green turtle soup, olives, martinis, broiled sweet bread, mushrooms, coffee frappe, filet of beef, sweet potatoes, green peas, Bethel Inn salad, vanilla ice cream, hot chocolate sauce, and, finally, assorted cakes and coffee.[218]

Following the bountiful meal, remarks by William Bingham 2nd and others were heard. Dr. Gehring was recorded as speaking "to us most impressively, inspiring us with fresh courage as we go forth to our various pursuits."[219] Songs, written for the occasion, were sung. The assemblage then adjourned across Broad Street to William J. Upson's "attractive little theatre," where a pantomime, two dances, plus a charade acting out the word "Gehring," were presented.[220] Another evening religious service in the Gehring's spacious drawing room was held, followed the next morning by a business meeting of the League at the Bethel Inn.[221] The next meeting of the group was scheduled for September 15-16, 1916.

On September 14, 1916, Dr. and Mrs. Gehring, who had been traveling outside New England, were met at the Bethel railroad station by a "coach and four, loaded with welcoming friends and driven by Mr. Fuller, who proved himself more than equal to his fiery steeds!"[222] That evening, the Gehrings hosted an informal reception at their Broad Street home. It was described in the local newspaper as the place "where the welcome hospitality, which is always such a large part of the entire work, was again dispensed by Mrs. Gehring, and where many pleasant acquaintances were made and renewed."[223]

The following day, due to rain, the afternoon tea was held at the Bethel Inn rather than at the Songo Pond camp. As the newspaper report lamented, "a certain picnic element was lost" with this adjustment, but the blazing fire in the Inn's music room fireplace, plus the "exquisite decorations of wild clematis" more than made up for the professed loss.[224] A dance in the evening, with its offering of songs and stories, "aroused much merriment."[225]

Prior to the annual meeting the next day, members of the Bethel League were involved in a number of activities, including golfing, motoring, and just plain walking. After lunch, the League meeting was called to order by Miss Lawrence, the vice president, in the absence of Mrs. Faulke, the president. William J. Upson, the secretary, delivered his report, and Will Bingham, the Treasurer, indicated that the funds previously collected more than covered the expenses of the reunion. All the officers were re-elected, and a nominating committee was selected to secure a president for the coming year.

During the evening's banquet, thirty-five members of the League—the largest yet assembled—gathered around "a table beautifully decorated with quaint, branchings of candlesticks of birch bark, and a center piece of delicate flowers."[226] Besides the traditional songs, a new piece written by Miss Helen Tetlow, titled "Drink to me only with hot milk," was predicted in the newspaper report to become "a League classic."[227] At the end of the meal,

telegrams from Mrs. Faulke and various other League members
were read. Dr. Gehring then addressed the group with a prepared
paper that was already anticipated to be the equivalent of a "keynote
address."[228]

Gehring's speech was not quoted in this news account and is
presumably lost. However, the reaction to his remarks underscore
the high esteem in which he was held by all those present. This
response can be summed up in the words of the newspaper account:

> If ever there was a happy, healthy, well poised gathering it was
> the one which listened thankfully and reverently to the words of
> him to whom they owed their new strength and courage—to
> him whose patience had never failed, whose hand had upheld
> them on the roughest road, whose understanding had made it
> possible for them to lay their burdens at his feet—him to whom
> his friends accord that beautiful title became [sic] by another dis-
> ciple of the same Master—"The Beloved Physician."

Will Bingham's arrival in Bethel in 1911 with his friend William
J. Upson in search of Dr. Gehring's "miraculous therapies" occurred at a propitious time for him and for the town, which, in 1910,
was recorded as having 1,930 residents. Will's response to the
Doctor and his wife was most positive, although it is unclear exactly
what therapeutic treatments were initially prescribed for him. In any
case, Will appeared to almost immediately believe he was in the
"right" hands and in the "right" place. Indeed, it seems likely that
he finally was—especially in light of his strained relationship with
his own father. Will was clearly looking for a friendlier, more genial
"father figure," and Dr. Gehring seemingly fit this role well. In
addition, because the early death of his mother had left a deep void
in Will's life, it is plausible that someone as formidable as Mrs.
Gehring could easily have had a profound influence upon the thirty-
two year old former Clevelander.

Another significant—and surely positive—influence upon Will at this time was Mrs. Gehring's older half-sister, Mary True (1845-1919), who was a highly successful teacher of the deaf. Her most famous student was Mabel Hubbard (1857-1923), the hearing-deprived daughter of Gardiner Hubbard, a founder of the National Geographic Society, and, due to his daughter's disability, a pioneer in education for the deaf.[229] Mabel Hubbard would later marry Alexander Graham Bell (1847-1922), inventor of the telephone and one of the leading figures of the late nineteenth and early twentieth centuries.[230]

After a very distinguished career in Boston and in other parts of the nation, Mary True retired to her hometown of Bethel and lived with her brother, Alfred, a Civil War veteran, in a Broad Street house she called "The Delinda," after a former owner.[231] Miss True, along with other Broad Street residents, rented rooms to Dr. Gehring's clientele. It was at Mary True's residence that Will Bingham lived for several years prior to the purchase in the 1920s of his own home on the other side of the street. Alexander Graham Bell and his wife, Mabel, stopped each year in Bethel on the way to their summer home in Nova Scotia to visit her old teacher. It is likely, then, that Will Bingham met this famous couple while he was a boarder at Miss True's. What is more, both Will's father and his sister, Frances, became friends with Miss True and often requested that they be remembered to her in their letters to Will. In the fall of 1914, Mary True visited Cleveland, and Frances Bolton arranged a luncheon there in her honor.[232]

The same summer that Will Bingham came to Bethel, the Prospect Inn, owned by Mrs. C. F. Lord and leased by the Frank R. Greene Company with Harry King as Manager, partially burned on July 22, 1911.[233] It was soon made public that the hotel, which had fronted the south side of the Bethel Hill common since 1863, would not be rebuilt. That announcement attracted the interest of Bethel's famed music conductor, "Professor" William Rogers Chapman (1855-1935), who, in 1897, after years in New York City, founded the Maine Music Festival with Mrs. Gehring's able assistance and organizational capabilities.[234] Held annually, the Festival was made up of choruses from throughout Maine, plus outstanding singers and orchestras with national and international reputations. It continued to attract audiences until its demise in 1926, due to its inability to compete with the growing popularity of the radio.

There is no evidence that Will Bingham ever attended a performance of the Maine Music Festival, but with his connection to Mrs. Gehring and his well-known fondness for all things musical, he certainly must have been aware of the festival's existence. Moreover, W. R. Chapman sometimes enticed several of the celebrities who graced the Festival to visit him in Bethel and perform in Odeon Hall, a spacious public venue on the second floor of Main Street's Cole Block. Among those who accepted Chapman's invitation was Metropolitan Opera star Geraldine Farrar, who appeared there in 1909, two years before Will's arrival.[235]

In early August 1911, W. R. Chapman made an announcement in the local newspaper that he had purchased the former Prospect Hotel property and, with several others, would soon build a new, elegant hotel designed by a Boston architect to replace the old one.[236] Toward the end of August, the citizens of Bethel held a special town meeting, and as an incentive to construct a new hotel facility, approved a motion allowing the land to be exempted from taxation for ten years, provided that a hotel costing more than $25,000 would be constructed.[237]

It is not clear why Professor Chapman's group did not move ahead with construction of a replacement for the Prospect Hotel. Very likely the reason was largely financial. In any case, nothing seems to have transpired about erecting a new hotel until later the following year. In November 1912, the Bethel Inn Corporation was formed with the following stockholders: Horace Sears, Robert Winsor, and Charles W. Hubbard, all from the Boston area; "William Bingham II" and William J. Upson of Cleveland; and Dr.

John George Gehring of Bethel. The officers of the newly formed corporation were: President, John G. Gehring; Vice President, Horace Sears; and Secretary-Treasurer, Ellery C. Park, Bethel Attorney.[238] All of the above individuals, except for Ellery Park, were former patients of Dr. Gehring. It was this new corporation that acquired the former hotel lot from Chapman and began construction of what would become the Bethel Inn. Work commenced without delay in November 1912 and continued through the winter. By May 1913, the structure was nearly completed.[239] The stockholders had provided for over half the cost, and William Bingham and William J. Upson agreed to assume all further financial obligations that arose. On July 8, 1913, the new Bethel Inn, designed by the Boston architectural firm of Coolidge and Carlson, opened to the public with Philip B. Young as manager.[240] Nearly four years later, a bronze plaque custom-made by Tiffany of New York was placed over the lobby fireplace by the incorporators of the Bethel Inn in honor of Dr. John George Gehring.[241]

The opening of the Bethel Inn in 1913 provided housing for many of Gehring's clientele and also added a quality hotel to the scene for the convenience of other Bethel visitors. Over the next few years, numerous changes and improvements were made to the Bethel Inn to enhance its popularity with the traveling public and to provide high quality facilities for a variety of activities. Among these was the addition of tennis courts and a golf course in 1915.[242]

In 1915, a residence across Broad Street from the new Bethel Inn was added to the holdings of the Bethel Inn Corporation. This house and barn had been constructed in the 1850s by David Hammons, who once represented Maine in the U.S. House of Representatives. The property was later owned by a Boston liquor merchant, A. T. Rowe, who sold it to the Bethel Inn. Thereafter, the house was occupied by William J. Upson, Will's friend and partner in the Bethel Inn. It was Upson who paid to have the former Hammons barn remodeled into a theater that was added to the

Inn's facilities. Used as an entertainment center for piano recitals and vocal performances, the theater featured a small, but attractive stage, plus dressing rooms for Gehring's patients and others, who acted in well-attended plays and pageants.[243]

William J. Upson was born in Unionville, Connecticut, in 1878 and educated there and in Cleveland, Ohio, where he presumably became acquainted with Will Bingham. The two men came to Bethel seeking assistance from Dr. Gehring; both found the community very agreeable and soon became residents of the town. In 1919, Upson married Nina Hodgdon of Orland, Maine; she had been born in that town in 1879, and thus was the same age as Will Bingham. It is unclear how Upson met her, but Nina Upson lived on in the house across from the Inn until her death in 1955 (also the year of Will Bingham's passing). William J. Upson died in 1936, and both he and his wife are buried in Bethel's Woodland Cemetery, along with the Gehrings, the senior George Farnsworth, Mary True, and Dr. Nathaniel Tuckerman True. The Upsons had no children. In his obituary, it was recorded that William J. Upson was "modest and retiring" and that he "loved music and reading," which must have been two of his bonds with Will Bingham.[244] Upson was active in town affairs, serving as a Trustee of Gould's Academy, joining the Board the same year as Will Bingham (1917). He also was an incorporator of the Bethel Savings Bank and spent many years as a trustee of the Bethel Library Association.

Less than a year after his arrival in Bethel, Will Bingham made his first financial commitment to Gould's Academy, undoubtedly at Mrs. Gehring's behest, as she was beginning to encourage her husband's patients to create an endowment for the Academy—her beloved father's old school. Will pledged $2500, and his friend, W. J. Upson, $1000.[245]

Involvement in the community and at Gould's Academy clearly appealed to Will at this important time in his life. An item in the local newspaper for October 1912 recorded that Will was featured as one of several performers at an entertainment in Bethel's Odeon

Hall.[246] Two months later, in December 1912, Will was listed as having played his violin at a concert in the Congregational Church.[247] In September 1913, Will again played the violin accompanied on the piano by his sister, Frances, at a memorial service for Liberty Holden (1833-1913). An 1853 Gould's Academy graduate, Liberty Holden became its first major benefactor after a long and prominent career in Cleveland, particularly as owner of the *Cleveland Plain Dealer*.[248] A little over two years later, in December 1915, the local paper noted that Will performed two violin solos at the Academy during an event honoring the birthday of Morris Pratt, who had been a Gehring patient and had died following a year as a student at Amherst College. William J. Upson joined Will in this endeavor, singing with two others.[249]

Based on his performances at these musical occasions, it seems clear that Will Bingham was at least somewhat comfortable appearing before diverse audiences during this stage of his life. As well, his interest in the Bethel Inn and nearby Gould's Academy helped sustain his general interest in the community. Following the death of his uncle, Oliver Hazard Payne, on June 27, 1917, things began to change again for Will, especially when news reached him that he was to receive one tenth of his late mother's brother's estate—reputably one of the largest in the nation at that time. Even before this momentous event, however, Doctor and Mrs. Gehring certainly had expectations that Will might be useful in meeting some of the Academy's needs, as it began to face an uncertain future due to declining enrollment and income. Will's early gift in 1912 of $2500 toward an endowment fund had surely given them encouragement. Five years later, in the fall of 1917, Will was elected to the Academy's Board of Trustees and again made several generous contributions, including the promise of an annual gift of $1800 to the cash-strapped institution. Yet, despite his interest in the Academy's wellbeing, he attempted to resign as a trustee in 1918, but his resignation was not accepted. Consequently, he continued to serve as a trustee for the rest of his life, though as far as one can tell, he never attended a single board meeting.[250]

As unpresumptuous and limited as his initial interest in the Academy appeared, it soon became clear (undoubtedly through the Gehrings' influence) that Will was even now considering certain significant plans for upgrading the school's facilities and placing the institution on an increasingly solid financial footing. Among these improvements were adding a central heating plant, renovating the dormitory and classroom buildings, and possibly constructing a gymnasium.[251] To underscore his commitment at this time, he made a $10,000 gift to the Academy's endowment.

By the spring of 1919, the Academy was facing such a bleak future that longtime Principal Frank E. Hanscom (1863-1940) despaired for its future; at the same time, Mrs. Gehring was deeply concerned that her father's beloved school might face extinction without a generous infusion of cash. Fortuitously, the $10,000 Bingham gift to the endowment was soon followed by an encouraging announcement spelling out plans for a gymnasium, a domestic science building, a provision for more faculty hiring, and an overhaul of the Academy's main classroom building. Suddenly, there appeared to be no limit to Will Bingham's generosity toward the Academy. He even proposed a special meat or milk fund, a proposition that Principal Hanscom welcomed on behalf of the students.[252] Of course, it is evident that none of these major developments would have been achieved without the influence of Doctor and Mrs. Gehring, and their close collaboration with Will Bingham. Other key players in the cultivation effort for this signal donor were Gould's Principal, Frank E. Hanscom, and Bethel attorney Ellery C. Park (1864-1949), longtime Gould Trustee and adviser to Will Bingham, who would serve many years as Treasurer and Supervisor of Buildings and Grounds for the Academy.

Throughout his earliest involvement with Gould's interests, Will also faced a number of personal issues. The United States entered World War I in April 1917. A conscription draft was soon announced for the nation, and the local newspaper contained an item listing Will's name among the fifty-five potential draftees.[253] In response to this news, it was decided that Dr. Gehring would be asked to write a letter to authorities stating that Will Bingham should be excused from service due to health issues, an exemption that was approved.[254] In light of the patriotic fervor of that era, however, Charles Bingham urged his son to buy Liberty Bonds and support the war effort financially. In Bethel, there was a campaign to produce additional food for the war effort, and every able-bodied man was encouraged to plant one acre of hoed crops to prevent food shortages caused by the conflict.[255] A food conservation movement in Bethel also was formed with 340 families, including Will Bingham, pledging to restrict their consumption. Local support for "our boys," in addition to Liberty Bonds, included the creation of knitted items to make life on the front more endurable. Sweaters, mufflers, wristers, socks, and helmets were in much demand. Will Bingham and William J. Upson were recorded as the chief suppliers of funds to purchase wool yarn for these items. Upson even took the extra step of providing cash prizes for those who produced the most knitted items between October 1917 and Easter 1918.[256]

By the summer of 1918, Will Bingham had made up his mind to give up his Cleveland residency to become a citizen of Bethel. In a letter dated August 16, 1918, to the Board of Selectmen, he wrote, "[I have] changed my domicile from Cleveland to Bethel, Maine where I have been living practically for over six years and where I will now vote and pay my pole [sic] and personal property taxes."[257] This decision to change domiciles was not done easily, for Will was concerned about sentimental attachments, his family's reaction, and that in Maine, "a state that is not very wealthy, my tax return would loom up astonishingly large, not so much this year as later."[258] In response to these worries, Charles Bingham urged his son "strongly to make the change," since he could "easily resume residence" in Cleveland again "if desirable."[259] Furthermore, he did not think that the tax situation should be a consideration since Will was "practically now a Maine resident."[260] He stressed to his son that he appreciated "the sentiment connected" with the change, but "did not think it should be considered now."[261]

Will's reliance upon his father's counsel underscores a dependence on the advice of strong personalities that was a pattern throughout his life. This dependence on others undoubtedly began with his father, but that paternal role was in many ways absorbed by Dr. Gehring. Surviving correspondence between the Doctor and Will from late 1912, while he was briefly away from Bethel and back in Cleveland to attend a wedding, is quite revealing in this respect. For example, a letter from October 1912, addressed to "my dear Billy," thanked Will for providing a "glimpse of your state of mind and obvious well-being."[262] Gehring admitted that both he and his wife had "long been sighing and wishing for a note from you." The Doctor, with tongue in cheek, noted that Mrs. Gehring "has been most solicitous to have you develop symptoms that required your immediate return."[263] Contrariwise, Marian True Gehring had confessed "to a feeling of gratification that you are so well and able to leave the family nest."[264] Both of them, Dr. Gehring wrote, were "rejoicing at your well being" and yet focusing on "a relapse to bring you back for our own sake."[265] Apparently Will had written Dr. Gehring about some mental state that had begun to trouble him, but he had ostensibly overcome the condition—at least for the present. Of this, Gehring wrote, "I haven't the slightest doubt but what the bubble has been pricked, however, and the gas let out, and [I] want you to do the very same thing again to me by letter should any other occasion present itself."[266] In a communiqué from November 1912, Gehring thanked Will for discussing his latest mental state, which focused on some disturbing dreams.[267] Gehring urged Will to take his subjective visions and "forget" them as fast as they emerged, "and have a good time."[268] When things got a bit serious, the Doctor advised Will not to "neglect to occasionally use your friend the Elixir Valeriante, and it might be a good plan if you are bothered, to resort to two or three grains of Calomel at bedtime once in awhile," adding that "these will put a new face upon things, should you get troubled."[269] Two weeks later, Gehring wrote Will that he was "glad you are wisely resorting to the little medical aids which I have equipped you, and thereby cross any little gullies that may happen along."[270]

Although Will Bingham did not serve in World War I, several members of his family did, including his brother Harry and his brother-in-law, Chester Bolton. Instead, as previously mentioned, Will made a donation of $150,000 for Liberty Loans to finance American participation in the war; he also donated $50,000 to the Red Cross.[271] At first, Will wanted to make his donations anonymously, but his father, Charles, insisted they be under his son's name.[272] Reluctantly, Will yielded to his father's influence, his gifts helping Charles Bingham reach his quota for the drive.

One of the other expressions of Will's generosity during the "Great War" was the donation of horses to the U.S. Army for his brother Harry's benefit and use. This endeavor took some persistence to overcome bureaucratic obstacles, but was eventually accomplished. Throughout the war, Charles Bingham forwarded Harry's letters on to Will. Furthermore, his sister, Frances, had high praise for Will's financial support of the war effort. Writing to Will in November 1917, she declared, "I am tremendously proud of you, Bing, and I just must say it!"[273] Later in the letter, she speculated, "I have a hunch, old Boy, that you have been feeling pretty much irked over not getting into an action part of the game."[274] This latter sentiment was undoubtedly misplaced since, by August of the following year, Will was reporting to his father that Dr. Gehring's advice was to avoid combat, and that Bethel physician, Dr. I. W. Wight, the medical officer for Oxford County working with Attorney Ellery Park, was seeing to his compliance with the new draft law to remain ineligible for military service.[275]

Will's brother, Harry, joined his sister, Frances, in praising Will's substantial financial support of the war. Harry also informed

Will by letter that their father had returned home after "a pleasant visit" to Maine, and that Charles Bingham was impressed "with many stories of your popularity in and around Bethel."[276]

Besides making financial contributions to the war effort and adhering to draft laws during this time, Will Bingham's attention was focused on the transfer of his Uncle Oliver's sizeable assets to his holdings—always under the watchful eye of his father, who frequently offered useful advice and cautious guidance. The receipt of this substantial bequest took nearly two years to complete and raised concerns for Will regarding his tax liability. Thankfully, these anxieties were for the most part assuaged through the sage advice of his father, Charles, and the Wall Street broker F. S. Rollins.

Following the Armistice of November 1918 that ended the Great War, and possibly to escape some of the winter chill in Bethel, Will decided to take a train journey in January 1919 from Bethel to Santa Barbara, California, with a side trip to the Grand Canyon. The private car *Philadelphia* left Bethel on January 15, 1919, with Will and six others (presumably men) on board. According to the Grand Trunk Railway System invoice for this excursion, there was no liquor requested, but Poland Spring Water, plus several brands of ginger ale, were available to the travelers. In addition, two types of cigarettes and 150 cigars had been supplied. Based on the logged itinerary, the party arrived at the Grand Canyon on January 20 and left the following day for California. For a trip that lasted fifteen and one-half days—January 15 to January 30—the final cost was given as just over $3,500, which included war taxes.[277] Prior to making this trip, Will was assured by his father that an envelope to be opened only by Charles Bingham or other family members in the event of his (Will's) death or "incapacitating illness" had been received and was safely sequestered in Charles's safety deposit box in Cleveland's Citizens Savings and Trust Company.[278]

Will undoubtedly met Dr. George Bourne Farnsworth, Jr. (1880-1947), Mrs. Gehring's son from her first marriage, through his close connection to the Gehrings. In fact, surviving documents suggest that Will may have become acquainted with Dr. Farnsworth and his wife, Ruth, prior to the visit he made to Cleveland in the fall of 1912. Except for the time of his service during World War I, George Farnsworth resided and practiced medicine in Cleveland from 1910 to 1930. In any case, their meeting would not only have important significance for Will's later life, but it had more immediate weight in providing conceivably favorable circumstances for Dr. Farnsworth (eventually "Captain" Farnsworth) to request funds from Will in 1917. "I make no apology for asking [for] a contribution from you, tho [sic] I am well aware your past generosities have been boundless," Farnsworth wrote. "But I am face to face with a great need," he explained. Farnsworth had "a hundred homesick, friendless, scared drafted men" in his command, and expected "one hundred more to join them" at Camp Sherman in Chillicothe, Ohio. With a sense of urgency, he continued, "I have done all I can from my own pocket, and the morals of these men are at stake."[279] It can be assumed that this request was answered, but Will Bingham's official response has not been located.

Once the Great War was over in November 1918, war relief and reconstruction became of vital interest to many Americans, led perhaps most notably by the example of Herbert Hoover, who headed the American Relief Administration in 1919 and 1920. In Will's case, he had been solicited for support as early as the fall of 1916 by Professor Samuel T. Dutton of Teachers College, Columbia University in New York; Dutton summered at Douglas Hill, Sebago, Maine, not far from Will's residence in Bethel. As secretary of the America Committee for Armenian and Syrian Relief, and treasurer of Constantinople College, an American College for girls in Constantinople (today's Istanbul), Professor Dutton approached Will for financial assistance to benefit post-war reconstruction and female higher education in the Near East. Starting with a $10,000 gift for wartime relief and other smaller donations to Constantinople College, Will increased his commitment in 1922 with the gift of $500,000 for a hospital build-ing for women at Robert College in Istanbul in memory of his mother.[280] Will turned out to be a very generous donor, indeed, to Near East causes and did serve briefly on the Board of Robert Col-lege; as in the case of Gould Academy, however, he probably never attended a meeting of the trustees.

At about the same time Will was dealing with these Near East beneficiaries, he was also working with Bethel's authorities on fire protection for the Bethel Inn. Throughout his life, Will appeared almost obsessed with the potential danger of fire. Thus, it was no surprise that whenever he donated buildings in numerous places throughout the world, one of his major interests was the installation of sprinkler systems and the use of fire proof construction materi-als.

Will Bingham's presence in Bethel also brought invitations from those connected with the Bethel Water Company for him to acquire some of the stock of that entity. Ellery Park's law partner, Judge Addison E. Herrick (1847-1932), who served as Secretary and Treasurer of the Bethel Water Company, urged Will to buy the firm's stock "to keep the ownership of the Co. in the hands of Bethel men who will wish to consider the interests of the community as well as that of the company."[281]

It remains unclear whether Will actually acquired any Bethel Water Company stock, but he may well have. What is known for sure is that in 1924 he did something even more significant by purchasing—for $50,000—approximately 2500 acres of forest land to ensure that the watershed of Chapman Brook, the source of Bethel's drinking water, was protected from adverse encroachments.[282] The deed, dated October 22, 1924, stated that the purchase was intended to "convey all the land lying in the Chapman Brook Valley which is now owned by said Penley Brothers Company and which drains into said Chapman Brook Valley."[283]

Five months later, on March 30, 1925, Will transferred his 2500 acres of Chapman Brook Valley land to the Bethel Water Company. According to the deed of gift, Will stated that it was his "desire and purpose to provide and insure a permanent and perpetually protected source of water supply for said Bethel Village and the community and territory which may be naturally, reasonably and safely served."[284] He further stipulated in this deed that "the tree and forest growth of all kinds upon said tract shall be forever conserved."[285] The document continued, "Nothing shall ever be done upon or in connection with said tract of land, which may interfere with, endanger, injure or pollute the water taken therefrom."[286] Will's deed to the Bethel Water Company did allow for some "judicious" timber harvesting to pay property taxes, but stated that if the land ceased to be the source of the municipal water for the town, it was to be transferred to the State of Maine.[287] And if the State did acquire the land, it would be designated and maintained as "a public game preserve, bird or game sanctuary, public park or State Forest Reserve."[288]

That eventuality came to pass in July 2007 when a violent rain and wind storm filled the reservoir on Chapman Brook of the Bethel Water District (successor to the Bethel Water Company) with trees, rocks, and soil, thus rendering it unusable for supplying the Town of Bethel with water. Following this catastrophe, it was decided to change the source of municipal water to newly-driven wells west of Chapman Brook. This decision meant that the provisions placed in the deed in case Chapman Brook was no longer the source of the town's water were activated. The State of Maine temporarily became the guardian of Will Bingham's gift, but the State soon relinquished its rights, transferring the responsibilities for carrying out Will's intent to the Town of Bethel. By a majority vote at the Bethel town meeting on January 30, 2013, the parcel was placed under the supervision of a newly created "Bingham Forest Authority," which will oversee restricted outdoor recreation, the maintenance of sustainable yield timber harvesting, use of the acreage for wildlife habitat, and utilization of the property as a back-up water supply if needed. Faithful to Will Bingham's vision, all these uses will be closely regulated in order to follow his 1925 directive that the watershed be managed in ways that will protect the water quality of Chapman Brook and its tributaries.

In addition to securing protection for Bethel's water supply, several other significant developments in Will's life occurred during the 1920s. Certainly a significant event was his purchase of a modest Shingle Style house on Bethel's Broad Street, just north of the Gehrings in 1922; still standing in excellent condition at the time of this writing, Will's new home was soon afterward extensively expanded and remodeled under the supervision of the Boston architectural firm of Coolidge and Carlson—the company that had designed the Bethel Inn a decade earlier. Another incident which had a profound effect upon Will in the early 1920s was the appearance of an article in a Boston newspaper announcing that the wealthiest person in Maine resided in Bethel—something that Will had, earlier in a letter to his father, feared would someday happen. This unwanted publicity had the effect of driving Will into isolation, thereby ending the days when he could stroll casually around Bethel's streets, play his violin at various community gatherings, and dance with Bethel women.[289]

Even before the Boston article appeared, it's clear that word of Will's capacity to aid others financially had spread locally and, in actual fact, throughout much of Maine. As a result, some of the earliest pleas for financial support from Will Bingham foreshadow what was to become an exceedingly common state of affairs during his later life. For example, a "Mrs. R.C." of Bethel wrote to Will in February of 1916, inquiring, "Do you happen to know who looks after the poor of this town as there is a case of extreme poverty and destitution in East Bethel?" The author continued to inform Will that "there is a woman and two little ones [who] live here in a camp and I happen to know they are pretty badly off." She termed them "good worthy people," continuing, "I know she would starve rather

than let anyone know their circumstances." Requesting that he investigate this situation, she asked that he keep her inquiry
confidential.[290] No response to this letter has survived. Yet another
example from about this time, written by an individual seeking
funds for medical equipment, did receive a positive reply from Will.
It is significant that this plea occurred after Will received the Payne
bequest and inaugurates a pattern of interest by Will (who tended
toward hypochondria) in many things medical. Edward Perkins
Carter, a physician formerly of Cleveland, wrote Will from
Baltimore that he had accepted a University and Hospital
appointment in the Johns Hopkins University Medical School.[291]
Almost immediately, Carter found the electrocardiograph
equipment in the laboratory, known as "the Heart Station," in his
words, "sadly out of date."[292] He forewarned Will that he was
openly writing "a begging letter," stating that Will could either "read
it or not" according to his mood at the moment.[293] Doctor Carter
hoped Will would respond in the affirmative, "because of your
interest in good works and in me."[294] He requested $2500, and
added that "anything above" that amount "would provide a
contingent fund."[295] Obviously, Will was positively influenced by
this solicitation (perhaps in light of the Cleveland connection) for,
two weeks later, Dr. Carter gratefully acknowledged Will's
benefaction; although the amount was not specified, there was
reference to the establishment of a "William Bingham Research
Fund."[296]

A more intense solicitation for a project of considerable
complexity came about in the 1920s from Dr. Clifton D. Gray,
President of Bates College in Lewiston, Maine. For years, under the
tutelage of Gould Academy's Principal, Frank E. Hanscom—who
was presented with an honorary M.A. degree from Bates in 1899
and in 1931 would be awarded an honorary doctorate—there
existed strong ties between the Academy and the Lewiston liberal
arts college. Hanscom was a forceful advocate for Bates as a college
choice for Gould graduates, with an impressive number over the

years having taken his advice. Not only did Bates honor Hanscom, the college also bestowed upon Dr. Gehring an honorary doctorate (LL.D.) in 1923. With these outwardly favorable conditions and connections in place, President Gray gained some confidence in laying out a strategy to interest Will Bingham in his indoor athletic building project. Gray's inclination to attract Will to Bates' needs had at least one precedent, since earlier, in 1919, the previous Bates president, Dr. George Chase, had solicited funds from Will and received a $1000 check for, in the benefactor's words, "unusual needs of the college" and "to do something to help an institution of good recognition and recognized value."[297] Will added at that time that he wanted to visit Bates and meet President Chase. That meeting probably never occurred, but by 1922, Will was seeking more information, according to Frank E. Hanscom, about the "merits and needs of Bates College."[298] In a letter to Chase's successor, Dr. Gray, the Gould principal was hopeful that his endorsement would help the president's cause, but Will Bingham, in Hanscom's words, "never commits himself and cannot be hurried or forced."[299] The Gould principal added that Will "never gives until he has investigated a cause thoroughly."[300] Moreover, Hanscom observed, "He is one of the most conscientious of men I have ever known, and looks upon his great wealth as held in trust for the good of his fellow men."[301]

As Will contemplated what his role in Bates' indoor athletic building project would be, he continued to raise questions for President Gray. One query directed to Dr. Gray concerned the relationship between Maine's liberal arts colleges and the University of Maine. This question was either not answered or the response has not been preserved. Another question from Will concerned sex ratios at Bates and the role of religion in liberal arts colleges. President Gray reported that Bates possessed a sixty/forty ratio in favor of men. As to religion, the Bates president wrote Will that he would not, "if I know it, invite anyone to teach here if he is not actively in sympathy with the Christian faith."[302]

Principal Hanscom of Gould Academy was also active in suggesting other possible benefactors for Bates, including Will's Bethel Inn partner, William J. Upson, who, he wrote, "does not like to be solicited personally, but is very susceptible to suggestion."[303] In addition, Hanscom reported to Dr. Gray that Upson's wife, Nina, was "decidedly enthusiastic" and would write Mrs. William K. Vanderbilt, who had spent some time in Bethel, for a contribution to Bates.[304]

A further influence in the dynamics of the Gray-Bingham collaboration was, of course, the cordial relations between Dr. Gray and his wife and Dr. Gehring and his wife, Marian. There appears to have been, from their surviving letters, genuine warmth between the two couples, with the Gray's son also spending time with the Gehrings.

Toward the end of 1922, having received the news that Will had donated $500,000 to found a medical college in Constantinople, Turkey, the previous year, Dr. Gray began to make a strong plea to Will for endowment funds to benefit Bates College. It appears that the president impressed Will with his answers to his earlier questions and was rewarded with a $60,000 endowment gift for Bates in December 1922. In the letter to Dr. Gray presenting this donation, Will wrote that he was "becoming increasingly sympathetic with the general plans of Bates College for attaining its ideals, and with the high Christian standard of ideals themselves."[305]

Dr. Gray's success in securing support for the college's endowment from Will and others encouraged him to make yet another plea for his most urgent need at the time, an indoor athletic facility which would allow students to exercise despite the weather for their "all round development." In Dr. Gray's letters making his case for the new building, he cited the very inadequate facilities currently in place and the necessity of serving more students in better ways in order to balance their physical and mental education.[306]

Through much of 1923, Dr. Gray continued to employ a number of strategies to attract Will's support, including breaking down the building project into phases and components. However, by November of that year, facing the funding of a new girls' dormitory (the "Marian True Gehring Students' Home") at Gould Academy in Bethel, Will informed Dr. Gray that his financial resources "in the matter of educational undertakings" through 1924 were "considerably committed," and "I do not see my way clear to help at Bates."[307]

After a pause of several months, Dr. Gray's persistence was renewed the following year as he began to turn to Dr. Gehring for help in securing the funds for his much-needed building project. By this stage, the Bates president had raised some monetary support for the building, but needed a lead donor to break what he considered to be a financial impasse. Still, little progress was made on the Bates athletic building fundraising campaign after Will backed off giving because of his commitment to Gould Academy. In May 1924, Dr. Gehring assured President Gray that he (Gehring) did not "want to be the indirect agent for an appeal," but urged the college leader to implore Will to renew his interest in giving to Bates.[308] Dr. Gehring promised his "warmest support" for the college, which he termed "his stepmother by adoption," and praised Gray's work in advocacy on behalf of Bates.[309]

The following month nature intervened to make construction of the desired facility even more urgent. The old gymnasium caught fire and burned on June 2, 1925, under what was officially termed "mysterious" circumstances. This event strengthened President Gray's resolve to find a major donor to make the proposed athletic building a reality. It is difficult to assess just how this devastating fire affected the change in Will's inclinations. However, after the extensive deliberations that had already occurred over the previous year, and helpful advice from Dr. Gehring, who kept Dr. Gray apprised of Will's mental health condition, an announcement was made eighteen days after the fire of Will Bingham's gift of $150,000 for the athletic building.[310]

Ground for this building was soon broken. *The Bates Student* reported that the primary interest of William Bingham 2nd was to "have the building aid in the general program of health for the entire student body, rather than play an exclusive part in intercollegiate sports."[311] The student newspaper added that during the winter months the indoor athletic building would provide for greater development of intramural sports and "general student health."[312]

In a departure from the usual practice of the time, Will specified that both men and women should possess, in the words of *The Bates Student*, "equal privileges in the new building."[313] To make certain that women were given their "equal privileges," Will added another $35,000 for the construction and equipping of a women's shower and locker room.[314] When completed, this facility was declared, in the words of *The Bates Student*, "the finest of its kind in the country."[315]

All this good news was announced to a 1925 commencement audience by a triumphal President Gray. Will Bingham was assigned a reserved seat at the ceremonies, but, as was his custom, he did not attend. In his honor, however, an impressive bouquet of roses was placed in front of the empty chair. Later in the day, three undergraduate students traveled to Bethel and personally presented the flowers to Will. According to *The Bates Student*, he was deeply touched by this act of appreciation, and asked these representatives of the student body to convey his expression of gratitude to their fellow undergraduates.[316]

Even with the funds now in hand, there remained one issue that had to be settled relating to this addition to the Bates campus: the name of the building. To President Gray, it was obvious that the major donor ought to be recognized through this naming opportunity. Consequently, in the fall of 1925 several letters were exchanged between Dr. Gray and Will on the naming issue. Dr.

Gray very logically proposed placing Will's name on the building, but the Bethel philanthropist categorically rejected that idea and countered with the suggestion of the "Clifton Daggett Gray Athletic Building."[317] President Gray's response underscored his gratitude for Will's suggestion, but reaffirmed his belief that the facility should bear the donor's name.[318] Nevertheless, by mid-November 1925, Dr. Gray had yielded to Will's reluctance to approve the use of his name. In a letter to Gray that reveals Will's tendency toward self-effacement, he expressed how "delighted" he was that the Bates Board of Trustees had enthusiastically approved naming the structure for its president.[319]

Along with the naming issue, there was some discussion of adorning a wall in the new athletic facility with a quote from Dr. Gehring's 1923 book, *The Hope of the Variant*. Dr. Gray expressed his enthusiasm for this addition to Will, especially since Dr. Gehring was an honorary graduate of Bates.[320]

One final matter faced by Dr. Gray in connection with the new athletic building was his invitation to Will to wield the silver trowel at the laying of the cornerstone. Predictably, with his increasingly strong aversion to personal publicity, Will declined the honor. Nonetheless, Dr. Gray sent Will the trowel with the suggestion that he might use it as a letter opener. (Dr. Gray's idea was actually adopted by the philanthropist, according to a surviving letter to Dr. Gray from Maria Pease, Will's nurse at the time.)[321]

Throughout this campaign, President Gray was in constant communication with Dr. Gehring, who, as Will Bingham's trusted advisor and physician, provided sage reports on his client's health, moods, preferences, and inclinations. Moreover, it must be acknowledged that Gehring himself was very favorably disposed toward the athletic building project and clearly guided the Bates president on matters of strategy, timing, and preferences, which immeasurably advanced the cause.

Two other major gifts made by Will in the 1920s in honor of his father, Charles Bingham (Yale '68), are worthy of mention here.

In 1926, to mark his father's eightieth birthday, Will and his surviving siblings gave Yale University the funds to build a dormitory (Charles W. Bingham Hall) enclosing the southeast corner of Old Campus, home of the original buildings that formed Yale. Designed by architect Walter B. Chambers and completed in 1928, this Collegiate Gothic structure, built of Longmeadow brownstone and cast stone, was L-shaped with a nine story tower.[322] Renovated and updated since opening, the massive building remains a prominent landmark on the Yale campus.

At approximately the same time, Will matched his father's gift of $500,000 for the Charles William Bingham Mechanical Engineering Building at the Case School of Applied Science in Cleveland. This large structure cost $478,500 to build, with Will's contribution (in honor of his father) earmarked for its endowment.[323]

Significantly, the year 1926 also marked the closing of Dr. John George Gehring's celebrated Bethel clinic. Although he continued to serve Will as a principal advisor almost until the time of his death in 1932, Gehring was beginning to deal with serious health issues—among them circulatory problems that would eventually result in his sudden death from a heart attack (reportedly while in mid-sentence) in a Florida hospital.[324] Marian True Farnsworth Gehring survived her husband by four years, also passing away in Florida on December 20, 1936.[325]

In 1927, Will had honored Dr. Gehring with a $200,000 gift to construct a neurological wing at Presbyterian Hospital in New York in the Doctor's name. At the same time, he also established one million dollar trust funds, each, for the Doctor and Marian. As events unfolded, these funds eventually benefited others.

One final major gift made by Will Bingham during the Gehring era took place five years later, in early 1932, when he presented a $200,000 donation for endowment to the Santa Barbara Museum of Natural History.[326] Not surprisingly, Will held fond memories of his youthful visits to this southern California city and had already made smaller contributions annually, beginning in 1924. This latest act of benevolence was purposely made to provide an income equal to his previous annual cash advances to the Museum.[327]

※ 3 ※

Life under "King George"

DOCTOR JOHN GEORGE GEHRING'S DEATH on September 1, 1932, closed out a significant phase of Will Bingham's life. Gone was the kind and understanding "father figure" who was such a stabilizing force, gently guiding him through all kinds of moods, emotional disruptions, illnesses, and stresses. The intricate and protracted discussions surrounding the Bates College Athletic Building campaign testify to just how successful Gehring was in comprehending this complex man who had placed so much confidence in the Doctor's advice and temperament.

About two years before Dr. Gehring's death, the stage was set for George Bourne Farnsworth, Jr.—Mrs. Gehring's son by her first marriage—to assume the position of Will's chief advisor. Marian Gehring's first husband, George Bourne Farnsworth, had passed away on April 11, 1887, when his son and namesake was only six years old. Born in Roxbury, Massachusetts, on December 16, 1880, George, Jr., came to Bethel with his mother after the father's death to live with his maternal grandfather, Dr. Nathaniel T. True, who died on May 24, 1887, shortly after their arrival. George Farnsworth and his mother continued their stay with Dr. True's widow (and Mrs. Gehring's mother), Susanna Webber Stevens True (1827-1911), while he attended Bethel's District 15 School, just down Broad Street from his grandparents' house. From late 1891 to mid-summer 1893, he toured Europe with his mother. The following year, after they had returned to Bethel, his mother (now Marian Gehring) organized the George Farnsworth Tennis

Club in honor of her first husband; this fledging organization included several prominent Bethel citizens, plus Mrs. Gehring and her son. George Farnsworth, Jr., then attended Gould's Academy before entering Bowdoin College, where he received his A.B. in 1903 Magna Cum Laude. He graduated from Harvard Medical School four years later.

Following a year abroad and some additional medical training in Boston, George Farnsworth moved to Cleveland and established an obstetrics practice, while also assuming a professorship at the Western Reserve University School of Medicine. He served as a Captain in World War I, commanding Battery B of the 322nd Field Artillery (1917-18) prior to returning to Cleveland when hostilities ceased. There he remained until word reached him of Dr. Gehring's failing health. Soon thereafter, he retired from his Cleveland responsibilities to become Will Bingham's faithful overseer in his medical, educational, and philanthropic interests. Since the Gehrings had a summer place at Christmas Cove, in the town of South Bristol, Maine, Dr. Farnsworth decided to adopt that picturesque coastal village as his legal residence. There he owned a very large Shingle Style "cottage," and later purchased several adjoining, but more modest, bungalows for his overflow guests— including, on one occasion, Will Bingham himself. Farnsworth also added a circa 1790 Federal style house in nearby Damariscotta to his local holdings. Extensively remodeled and enlarged in a Colonial Revival vein, this "farmhouse" was subsequently dubbed "Farnstede Manor."

Dr. George Bourne Farnsworth was every inch his mother's son. Even though Marian True Farnsworth Gehring had grown up in Bethel, she pursued further education at Bradford Academy in Massachusetts and studied music in Boston, where she met her first husband. Following her return to Maine after the senior Farnsworth's death, and her subsequent marriage to Dr. John George Gehring in 1888, she seemed determined to regard herself as "the chosen one," her mission to instill culture and refinement into the local populace—particularly the youth of Bethel and the State of Maine as a whole. Accordingly, students at Gould's Academy, her father's old school, were regularly invited to her sumptuous Broad Street residence and subjected to sessions where they learned proper social manners and appropriate behavior through an organization called the Twentieth Century Club.[328]

Mrs. Gehring's social position in Bethel was maintained on such a high level that, to many who knew her, it appeared to resemble the trappings of royalty. For example, Dr. Samuel Proger recalled visiting the regal appearing Marian, along with a woman he termed her "lady-in-waiting" (Betty Burns Thurston) for what appeared "high tea."[329] He could not help but imagine that he had gone back a century or more in British history!

It is abundantly clear that Dr. Farnsworth, Mrs. Gehring's only child, learned these lessons of life all too well, and they were doubtless reinforced by his elite education at Bowdoin and Harvard. As a result, he was inclined to be controlling, arrogant, and self-important, although with the *proper* person he could be playful and downright genial. In his dealings with Will Bingham, he made sure to keep in close communication, tending to oversee every detail of the man's affairs. Consequently, there was none of the low-key "supervision" that Dr. Gehring had mastered, which gave Will the necessary support he craved; instead, Gehring's stepson exerted tight control over all of Will's activities, and on more than one occasion claiming for himself credit for financial gifts actually made by Will Bingham. As Dr. Farnsworth once declared to a headmaster at Gould Academy, in case there was any doubt as to his importance, "I am the Chairman of the Board of Trustees, I am Mr. Bingham's first representative and I employ Mr. Davidson [Will's attorney]." To this he added, brusquely, "Get this once and for all through your head."[330] Oddly, this declaration flies in the face of statements made in a letter penned by Farnsworth around the same time, where he proclaimed having "no knowledge whatever and no influence whatever in the secondary school field in Maine

EXCEPT at Gould Academy." He went on to explain that he had "knowledge," but "had I influence, I could not use it without detriment to the Headmaster, whoever he might be."[331] To make this assertion all the more emphatic, he continued, "The moment a member of the Board of Trustees tells the headmaster what to do with his teaching staff, at that moment, he ceases to be of value as a Trustee and becomes a menace to the institution."[332]

Moving to Maine from Cleveland and spending considerable time in the Bethel area, George Farnsworth became increasingly concerned with the level of competence exhibited by medical practitioners he observed first hand. As he recalled in 1931, he had brought to the attention of Will Bingham "the plight of the rural physician," pointing out how from the time of his graduation from medical school he "was cut off from the stimulating and developing contacts to which his urban brother was exposed."[333] Those influences were listed by Farnsworth as "progressive medical societies, hospitals, clinics and medical school teaching."[334]

To alleviate this medical dilemma, Farnsworth possessed a willing ally in Will Bingham, who was often—as has been previously stated—predisposed to all kinds of maladies, both real and imagined. It was only natural, then, that Will was sympathetic to the need for good rural medicine in Maine. The following year, in 1936, in the law office of Bethel attorney Ellery C. Park, the Bingham Associates Fund for the Advancement of Rural Medicine (B.A.F.), a Maine non-profit corporation, was created. Predictably, Will Bingham resisted having his name attached to this new enterprise at the outset, but he was finally persuaded by his associates. Doctors John G. Gehring, George Farnsworth, and Joseph Pratt (of whom, more) constituted the initial Board of Trustees. These physicians and Will, along with Ellery C. Park, Bertram L. Bryant, M.D., of Bangor (husband of Mrs. Gehring's sister, Lillian), and Fred B. Merrill, Bethel attorney and banker, comprised the Incorporators. Dr. Gehring was selected as the first president, but was soon succeeded by his step-son, Dr. George Farnsworth.[335]

The work of the B.A.F. commenced with the equipping of Maine's fifty-seven bed Rumford Community Hospital, located in a town bordering Bethel with, in Farnsworth's words, "everything it lacked."[336] These deficiencies were largely removed with the employment of a full-time technician, the creation of a pathology department, and the addition of the services of a resident M.D. from Boston. Clinics staffed by Tufts University Medical School professors were sponsored about once a month for country doctors to gain further knowledge and increased insight in their attempts to solve the most puzzling individual medical cases.

The timing of the creation of the B.A.F. was particularly opportune, as it became possible to move a diagnostic ward into a new structure in Boston owned by the century-old Boston Dispensary, which was a free clinic where Farnsworth's grandfather had studied in 1812. Dr. Farnsworth also obtained some of his medical training there nearly a century later in 1905. This diagnostic ward was located on one floor and was served by the laboratories of the dispensary. It also contained twenty beds, which were soon filled, with the average stay being about five days for diagnostic purposes only. Within four years, there existed a waiting list often numbering twenty patients or more.

In 1937, after considerable deliberation, the decision was made to build a sixty-five bed diagnostic hospital funded by the Bingham Associates Fund. Will Bingham provided $750,000 for the land acquisition and the building, and, once again, he declined to have his name attached to it. Instead, the honor went to his good friend Dr. Joseph Pratt, who had provided significant leadership for the project. Thus is was that the Joseph H. Pratt Diagnostic Hospital opened on December 15, 1938; at the time, it ranked as the nation's largest diagnostic medical facility.

Joseph Henry Pratt was born in Middletown, Massachusetts, on December 5, 1872.[337] After graduation from Yale's Sheffield Scientific School, he entered the newly-formed Johns Hopkins School of Medicine, graduating in 1898. At Hopkins, he came under the influence of their great faculty and made outstanding contributions in a number of medical fields, including internal medicine. Returning to Boston, Pratt served on the staff of Massachusetts General Hospital, where he made advances in tuberculosis treatment through group therapy. Building on this experience, he became focused on patients with psychoneurotic challenges, and achieved a formidable reputation for his work in this field of research. Serving as Physician-in-Chief of the Boston Dispensary from 1927, he amassed an outstanding record for medical innovations. A chance referral of Dr. Gehring to him, when Dr. Gehring began to suffer from angina in the spring of 1931, brought the two men together and soon resulted in a number of fortunate circumstances that would ultimately benefit the Boston Dispensary and its successors. Doctors Gehring and Pratt became close friends and for a brief time, with another physician, formed Gehring Associates in Bethel. It was into this arrangement that the Gehrings introduced Will Bingham and urged him to take Dr. Pratt on as his personal physician. As Will became increasingly aware of the needs of the Boston Dispensary diagnostic unit through his contact with Dr. Pratt, he began to assist financially. It was Mrs. Gehring who convinced Will to make an initial gift of $50,000 to equip the unit in 1931, and to provide an additional $20,000 for salaries and other expenses, if Tufts would expend $5000. In addition, Will also was persuaded to subsidize the unit's operating deficit to the extent of $2000 per month.[338]

Will's involvement in hospital construction projects actually preceded the B.A.F., since he had contributed generously to the building of the Rumford (Maine) Community Hospital in 1926 and underwritten additions to hospitals in Lewiston and Bangor, Maine. In 1927, as earlier noted, he donated $200,000 to fund a floor in the Presbyterian Hospital in New York named for Dr. Gehring. Undoubtedly through the influence of his sister, Frances, who served as a nurse in World War I and who took particular interest in the status of nursing throughout her long life, and possibly through the efforts of Near East education advocate Samuel T. Dutton, Will donated (as previously mentioned) $500,000 for a hospital in Istanbul connected to Robert College in memory of his mother, Mary Payne Bingham.[339] Given this background, the idea of upgrading current services in a hospital nearby that he had helped create in 1926 would have appealed to Will, and, thus, his enthusiasm for bringing "Boston to Maine," as it was popularly known, should not be surprising. Dr. Pratt and his associates began to work closely with Dr. Eugene McCarty, a much admired Rumford physician who served as one of the leaders in securing a modern facility for his community, to make the collaborative experience with the Boston Dispensary, and its successors, Pratt Diagnostic Hospital, and Tufts Medical School/New England Medical Center, a success.[340]

Early in this medical transition in Boston, the benefits for the Rumford Community Hospital's connection with the Boston Dispensary's diagnostic ward were clearly evident. Between November 1931 and November 1932 over 688 admissions were processed and 3826 days of care delivered. The Maine clientele kept the Dispensary's beds filled while at the same time the Rumford Hospital's personnel gained invaluable educational and diagnostic support.[341]

The physician Dr. Pratt recruited to oversee this unique "Boston to Maine" medical "alliance" was a doctor as strong in the laboratory as he was in medical practice, and one who had become increasingly involved in what became known as the "Rumford Program." Dr. Samuel H. Proger was a Southerner from Atlanta who had graduated Phi Beta Kappa at Emory University in 1925 and completed his medical education at Emory Medical School three years later with highest honors. He completed internships at New York's Bellevue Hospital and Atlanta's Piedmont Hospital.

At first, because serious administrative problems had developed at the Dispensary, Dr. Proger appeared inclined to accept an offer to do research and teach at his alma mater in Atlanta, Emory

University School of Medicine. When Dr. George Farnsworth received this news, he insisted that Dr. Proger be retained in Boston and proposed a five-year contract financed by Will Bingham that would prevent the talented physician from leaving New England. When Dr. Farnsworth informed Sidney W. Davidson, who had recently become Will's attorney and trustee, he immediately had an ally in his cause. Both Farnsworth and Davidson agreed that Dr. Proger was so essential to the success of Will's medical philanthropic interests that every effort needed to be made to keep Proger in Boston. This strategy was undoubtedly successful, since Dr. Proger did remain in New England. The suspicion from Dr. Farnsworth's and Attorney Davidson's perspective was that if Dr. Proger went elsewhere, it would likely have transferred Will Bingham's major charitable focus to other parts of the United States or even, perhaps, abroad.[342]

The five-year contract underwritten financially by Will Bingham solved the dilemma, and made it possible for Dr. Proger to spend the rest of his working life with the New England Medical Center. Here he became one of the outstanding figures in modern American medicine and contributed significantly to the reputation of Boston as a leading center for all things medical.

Once the Pratt Diagnostic Hospital was up and running, Dr. Proger insisted that it serve a larger purpose, one that became known as the Bingham Program. This innovative approach meant that small community hospitals could derive significant medical benefits from a larger metropolitan center on a regular basis. Furthermore, regional medical programs could be developed in Maine, with something like twenty communities receiving benefits along with the larger hospitals in Bangor and Lewiston. Among the advantages gained through the Bingham Program were diagnostic and laboratory services, equipment advances, continuing training of medical personnel, and the upgrading of facilities. For the most part, these services were supplied free of charge through Will's generosity. As their availability became better known and the lack of "strings" attached understood, more hospitals took advantage of these opportunities and the Bingham Program became a national model cited in 1944 by the Surgeon General of the United States.[343]

Two more significant contributions by Will to what became the Tufts-New England Medical Center should be noted. Both came after World War II and were largely due to the influence of Will's chief advisors of the era: Dr. Proger; Sidney W. Davidson, his attorney; Dr. Farnsworth; and Joseph Barr, engineer and builder. They settled on the proposition that a general hospital affiliated with Tufts Medical School would enhance the influence of the Pratt Diagnostic Hospital and draw prominent surgeons and highly qualified doctors to the institution, as well as strengthen its research capabilities and increase the possibilities of improved patient care. Several years of experience had made it clear that a team model of patient care with a group of doctors and other health professions was more likely to produce the preferred outcome. While the Pratt Diagnostic Hospital was considered outstanding in its handling of patients, the lack of a surgical unit was considered a deficiency, since it required moving the patient for surgery elsewhere. Within a general hospital, it was determined, patient care should remain comprehensive, without the need to transfer and possibly disrupt recovery.[344]

By 1946, Will Bingham was willing to assist in the financing of this new hospital building. However, financial difficulties involving the Boston Dispensary and its relationship with the Pratt Diagnostic Hospital required another corporate arrangement. The solution to this predicament was the creation of a new non-profit organization, the Bingham Associates Fund of Massachusetts, which came into being on July 1, 1947; it assumed "legal title of the Pratt" from the Dispensary following legislative approval.[345]

The plans for the new wing were approved by Dr. Farnsworth just prior to his death on May 22, 1947. Appropriately, the 150-bed "Farnsworth Surgical Building" was named for Will's chief advisor at the philanthropist's request. The cost of the structure was set at

$3,000,000. Half of this amount was dispensed by Will and his Trust for Charity, established in 1935 by attorney Sidney Davidson, who served as trustee of the Trust for Charity along with the United States Trust of New York. The remainder of the building funds needed for this project came from a First National Bank of Boston loan secured by assets loaned by Will. When the Farnsworth Surgical Building was officially opened on May 26, 1949, it was duly noted that it contained a number of innovative features, along with many hospital functions all under one roof.

Beginning in 1946, the Rockefeller Fund donated $250,000 that permitted the Bingham Associates Fund of Massachusetts to extend the Bingham Program to hospitals in the Connecticut River Valley. The Maine model served as an inspiration for the Bay State program, emphasizing improved medical care and post-graduate education opportunities for physicians in rural areas.

Following more than twenty years of close association with his patient, Dr. Proger left posterity a detailed description of Will Bingham that was composed soon after the great philanthropist's death in 1955.[346] Importantly, Proger's observations appear to be the most comprehensive of any that have survived. Among his recollections was that Will Bingham was a very complicated person, yet was easy to meet, as he was informal, genuine, wholesome, and unassuming. He could be friendly and was "thoughtful, pleasant and warm."[347] A casual meeting would provide little inkling that he was "in his own self-created and isolated world."[348]

Will's appearance, according to Dr. Proger, was "more dignified than imposing."[349] He noted his "quiet and gentle dignity," "his medium size with thin hair covering a fairly large head," and his "prominent brow and sharp blue eyes."[350] He described Will's conservative dress and his "deliberate" and "unhurried" manner.[351] According to Dr. Proger, Will "walked with almost military erectness."[352] There was at all times an "unobtrusive air of the aristocrat about him."[353] His memory was phenomenal, and he would meet with his advisors usually at ten in the morning and eight in the evening to discuss business and any medical problems. The balance of his day was spent eating his meals alone in his room, walking often with his nurse, and reading, with particular emphasis on adventure and nature.[354] Always extremely well informed, he remembered numerous minute details and never lost his sense of humor. Physicians who spoke with him had to be most precise in any statements they made to him.[355] Proger also believed Will possessed "a compelling desire to be helpful." [356] He was, according to the Doctor, "free of guile, absolutely incapable of deviousness, and completely honest."[357] Not surprisingly, he often focused on his health, and was overly concerned with what Dr. Proger generally considered non-existent or minor symptoms.

During Will Bingham's final illness, Dr. Proger tried to reassure him that tests indicated there was no serious disease, but he was not convinced, and Proger had no answer for this individual who faced crises with equanimity and was "completely secure in his spiritual strength."[358]

Dr. Proger was certain that Will took his philanthropic responsibilities very seriously, which helps explain his selfless concern for human welfare and his special traits of generosity.[359] He chose to be a recluse, even if it meant not seeing "members of his family who were dear to him and to whom he was deeply devoted."[360]

When Proger attempted to express his deep appreciation to Will for all his "magnificent support" to the Bingham Associates Fund and the New England Center Hospital, Will's reply was that he was the one to be thankful, since he "felt indebted and grateful for the opportunities that had been provided him to be helpful."[361]

While some of Will Bingham's focus in the 1930s was on major building projects in Boston and Bethel, he also lent his financial support to numerous humanitarian projects, such as one involving the widow of his father's second cousin, Mrs. Eliza Brown. Then living in Philadelphia, Brown suffered from glaucoma and was nearly blind in one eye. She required a constant companion—Ida

Bates Goff—was incapable of handling her finances, and spent what money she had extravagantly. Will attempted to get his siblings involved in Mrs. Brown's support, but Harry Bingham apparently did not respond, and his sisters only made modest quarterly contributions. Most of the burden of caring for Mrs. Brown fell upon Will and was directed by Dr. Farnsworth, who informed her companion, Miss Goff, in one letter "that it is my job to keep close supervision over those dependent upon Mr. Bingham," and, Farnsworth wrote emphatically, that "includes much more than merely sending out quarterly checks."[362]

The case of Mrs. Brown, whom Dr. Farnsworth described to Sidney Davidson as his "Philadelphia headache," was a complicated one, as Brown reportedly took heroin one time, was suicidal, addicted to codeine, and was definitely a trial for her companion.[363] Dr. Farnsworth tried to provide relief for Miss Goff, but with limited success. He did secure the services of a Philadelphia lawyer, Edmund Finnegan, to whom he deigned to express his love of "the Fighting Irish," to oversee her lease and other legal matters.[364] Farnsworth even had to rescue Mrs. Brown's jewelry (reportedly worth $2000), which she had pawned for cash.

Dr. Farnsworth's goal through the several years of involvement with Mrs. Brown was, as he expressed it to her companion, Miss Goff, to allow her to feel "dignified, quiet and comfortable."[365] He was constantly expressing his loss of patience with Mrs. Brown; for her part, Brown considered Dr. Farnsworth a "devil."[366]

By early 1940, Dr. Farnsworth was becoming weary of spending so much of his own time and Will's funds on Mrs. Brown, noting that "Mr. Bingham's money cannot be wasted on any one individual since he has to deny help to so many." Farnsworth's ordeal finally ended in May 1941 with Mrs. Brown's death, followed by her burial, for which Will was billed $477. In a letter to Will's nurse, Miss Boggs, Dr. Farnsworth expressed his satisfaction that everything that could have been done for Mrs. Brown had been carried out. The lawyer for her estate, Harold Ervin, contacted Dr. Farnsworth to inquire if Will intended to file a claim on her remaining assets, but Will declined, assuming that the probate expenses would absorb most of what little had been preserved of her estate.

Over a year later, after the distribution of Mrs. Brown's estate had been made, Dr. Farnsworth reflected upon the experience of his "Philadelphia headache," which he described in a letter as a "nightmare from the point of view of intelligent and responsible philanthropy." He recalled rescuing Mrs. Brown's jewelry and expressed the hope that those who received something from her estate were pleased, although he and Mr. Bingham did not come into "so much as a string of artificial pearls, despite the thousands squandered on her." He ended his letter, however, in a somewhat philosophical vein, expressing the view that ingratitude is the usual "lot of the philanthropist and his agent."

Around this same time, another situation involving an individual in dire need of financial help attracted Dr. Farnsworth's attention; fortunately, this case proved to be much less troublesome and closer to home. Dora Anthony, a music teacher in her seventies and a distant cousin of Dr. Farnsworth's wife, Ruth, had lost almost everything during the Great Depression of the 1930s and, with the onset of World War II, found her student numbers greatly diminished. Ruth Farnsworth moved her from New York City to Cleveland Heights, with the option of spending summers with the Farnsworths at Christmas Cove, Maine. In a letter to Will Bingham, George Farnsworth requested that he (Will) take her on in the event of his death, since Ruth would not be able to maintain her. By 1942, Will agreed to support her at an expense of $1800 a year, as Dr. Farnsworth was at that time obliged to support his daughter, Sally, and her husband, Neal Dale.

With the United States entry into World War II in 1941, financing the American forces became a paramount concern. Taxes on individual income rose markedly with the arrival of the Roosevelt administration in the 1930s, and became even steeper with the onset of the war, when higher taxes were imposed to fund approximately 46% of the war's expenses, with the rest being borrowed.[367] Of course, this higher taxation affected the amount of money Will Bingham had available to support his philanthropies. This circumstance was aggressively addressed repeatedly by Dr. Farnsworth, who complained bitterly about the situation, as in the case for the denial of funds to Colby College in Waterville, Maine. In a letter to E. W. Millett, Assistant Director of Physical Education at Colby, Farnsworth described the outlook as "dark" for philanthropies, and noted that Will was compelled to build two school facilities at Gould Academy "while he had the money and before income and capital should be taxed away from him."[368] As early as 1934, Will began to feel the burden of New Deal taxation. In a November 19, 1934, letter to his brother-in-law, Dudley Blossom, Will reported that he could not support the Cleveland Community Fund since "my philanthropic budget must be still further trimmed under last year to meet present economic conditions."[369] Dr. Farnsworth also underscored this emphasis on austerity in the 1930s in one of his letters to Opportunity Farm, a New Gloucester, Maine, charity dedicated to indigent youth. He warned officials there not to "expect the $1000 each year," since Will Bingham was reducing his support for what was described as "extraneous charities" in order to concentrate on his "major interests." Therefore, Farnsworth cautioned, it was necessary to avoid counting "your chickens before they hatch."[370] However, it appears that Will held a special regard for both Opportunity Farm and Good Will-Hinckley, two Maine-based charities. In a signed note to Dr. Farnsworth, he wrote, "In general, I would like to keep these people [Opportunity Farm and Good Will] on my annual budget."[371]

About 1933, Dr. Farnsworth and Will became increasingly concerned about the prevalence of tuberculosis in Maine. It was under the auspices of the recently created Bingham Associates Fund that June Hills Hunter, a social worker from Marblehead, Massachusetts, was engaged to work in Oxford County (primarily in the Rumford area) to eradicate this affliction from western Maine. Since she had been trained in Dr. Pratt's TB class, Mrs. Hunter, for the most part, had the complete confidence of Dr. Farnsworth, and his missives to her were generally friendly and often collegial, he addressing her in one letter as "you dear stiff-necked Mableheadite."[372] Will considered her letters and reports "refreshing, made interesting by her human way of putting things."[373]

The quest to eliminate tuberculosis in Oxford County sometimes led to assistance to stricken families in the form of a cow for milk, funds for dental work, or direct pay for the care of those in need. Neither Will nor Dr. Farnsworth appeared overly concerned that some of these financial commitments likely strayed from the primary focus of tuberculosis eradication. Possibly some of this leniency may have been due to the respect and indulgence they granted to Mrs. Hills for her dedication to duty and the thoroughness of her reports. Nevertheless, both Will and Dr. Farnsworth did not hesitate to make suggestions. For example, Will insisted that cows be tested for tuberculosis, and that Jerseys not be considered, as they don't "give as much milk as many other kinds," that their milk was "too rich for children," and that "they are particularly susceptible to t.b."[374]

Originally, Mrs. Hunter's work was tied to the Bingham Associates Fund's connection with the Rumford Community Hospital as, in Dr. Farnsworth's words, "an experimental station," with Dr. Pratt's recruitment of her as a social worker to "dig out cases of TB."[375] It was in Pratt's view, "only natural she came upon cases of destitution" during this quest.[376] Approximately $1000 was spent each year in what Farnsworth termed "uncontrolled charities in Rumford."[377]

Mrs. Hunter approached her work with great zeal and remarkable compassion, sometimes contributing her own funds to buy clothes for an impoverished high school student or assisting with other immediate expenses. In some cases, Will Bingham shared her compassionate spirit, which was particularly evident in the case of a farmer experiencing especially hard times during the Depression years. "We might be able to give him a boost if it does not run into much money and would look practical," Will wrote to Mrs. Hunter in an undated letter, adding "Let us find out how things stand anyway."[378]

In addition to helping others under Mrs. Hunter's care, Will also loaned Mrs. Hunter $2000 to fix up her Marblehead house so that it could be rented. Dr. Farnsworth questioned this action, but Will, in a handwritten note, approved it and stipulated that no interest payment be required.

Furthermore, Mrs. Hunter actively sought placement at Gould Academy for some of the students from the Rumford area that she encountered in her social work practice. Dr. Farnsworth assisted in this effort to a limited extent through his position as President of the Gould Board of Trustees and, of course, as Will's major advisor for philanthropic endeavors. Three sisters from Rumford were among those that Mrs. Hunter oversaw who attended Gould in the late 1930s with mixed results.

By 1939, Mrs. Hunter was experiencing pressure from the State Health Department, which was advancing the policy that all tuberculosis cases in Maine, including those in Oxford County, be reported and visited by State officials. Despite this ruling, the newly appointed head of the agency, Dr. Mitchell, was urging cooperation in the TB battle, to which Dr. Farnsworth made a marginal note in this section of Mrs. Hunter's letter, writing beside it: "Hell!"[379] In yet another note inserted in the margin, Farnsworth wrote, "yes indeed, petty jealousy a'plenty!"[380]

Not surprisingly, Mrs. Hunter was becoming discouraged and speculated that perhaps her current role was being taken over by the State. "Not so fast, my dear lady, not so fast!" was Farnsworth's response to her letter about ending work in fighting tuberculosis.[381] He proposed that she come to Bethel to work for the "brilliant young medical man" he was bringing to the town. So certain was he that the position was "made for her" that he declared she was "the only one for the job." To complete the recruitment exercise, he added, as an incentive, "You will like the intellectual atmosphere of Bethel in winter, I think."

Despite all of Dr. Farnsworth's enthusiastic support, Mrs. Hunter did not take the recommended position, but continued her tuberculosis eradication efforts and its attendant social welfare activities. Nonetheless, Dr. Farnsworth persisted in praising Mrs. Hunter, whom he found obviously attractive:

> I get quite a kick out of you! You are so much the stiff black Satin New England gentlewoman . . . and then you go and buy a black evening dress so that the girl may go to the dances! It is that broad human understanding side of you that breaks through the mold of your ancestry and flowers in an expression of deep human perceptions.[382]

One case that Mrs. Hunter spent considerable time on was that of Dale Mack, a talented teenager with tuberculosis who eventually went to Exeter Academy and was admitted to Yale. The details of his life are rather sketchy, but on one occasion, Dr. Farnsworth expressed his doubts as to whether Mack should travel abroad in the summer of 1939 or spend $400 on that trip. "He should be out-of-doors on a farm or a milk route or a counselor at a boy's camp all summer," Farnsworth wrote Mrs. Hunter, who apparently agreed.[383] Dale Mack also expressed interest in the Grenfell Mission in Labrador, which Dr. Farnsworth rejected as "too risky for him from a health standpoint."[384] Farnsworth went on to declare that "Maine is a perfectly good State for summer health," but, regardless of compensation, Mack needed "full daily occupation, not loafing or playing."[385]

Dale Mack attended Yale during World War II and contacted Mrs. Hunter that he had left some personal possessions in New Haven as he prepared to go into the U.S. Army—something that

Dr. Farnsworth had prophesized. He asked Mrs. Hunter if he could borrow the car she used in her work for the Bingham Associates Fund to travel to Connecticut for the purpose of retrieving these possessions. Mrs. Hunter attempted to clear this request through Dr. Farnsworth, but was met with a stern refusal. "Of course, Dale COULD NOT legally drive your car for any purpose whatever (without explicit permission) since the car is not your private car, but a car supplied you by the B.A.F. for particular work, in social service." Farnsworth continued, "Strictly speaking, I should not give him permission to drive it to New Haven and back, at any time at all and under the present rubber situation, I do not feel justified in using B.A.F. tires for such a private purpose." Furthermore, the Doctor asserted, "I fear Dale will have to pay for his thoughtlessness in leaving his things behind, by having to make a trip on the train or bus and expressing the things home." Because he had stated his sentiments so thoroughly and directly, Farnsworth added, "Sorry to be so hard-boiled, but I cannot justify any other action to my fellow Trustees. . . . In the event of an accident, I should personally have to pay for having a permit for use of a B.A.F. car by a private person. Sorry." What Mrs. Hunter thought of the Doctor's uncompromising decision is unknown.

Although there is no way of knowing whether Will Bingham was aware of Dale Mack's request for use of a B.A.F. vehicle, he did take an interest in the young man's medical problems. Will assessed the situation from a letter written by Mack to Miss Boggs, Will's longtime nurse, that she shared with her employer. Will found Mack's sense of well-being "particularly good" and praised his determination "to get well."[386] Stepping forward once again to assist someone he'd never met, Will directed Dr. Farnsworth to investigate to see if Dale Mack needed "a couple of suits of clothes and shirts and wardrobe generally."[387] He approved an expenditure of $100 if necessary.

Another case referred to Will by Mrs. Hunter was that of Ronald Scott, whom Will described as an "old t.b. case and first rate young man."[388] Scott, however, posed a dilemma for Will, who wrote, "I would like to help him and am willing to do so but not sure I want to help him keep a stand on the new road from Rumford to Rangeley where he will sell his berries, and I take it, farm products, probably also candies and drinks."[389] Will was worried about the "danger of spreading t.b."[390] With this concern in mind, he asked if there was "some other way" or if "something else could be found" to assist this individual.[391]

Clearly, in 1941 Mrs. Hunter was filled with enthusiasm as she toured the recently opened Farnsworth Field House at Gould Academy and met with Dr. Homer E. Lawrence, the new Gould physician.[392] At Dr. Farnsworth's suggestion, she had discussed tuberculosis with Dr. Lawrence in regard to the Gould student body, which Dr. Lawrence declared was "TB free," and she expressed the hope that "he would not need to call upon me."[393] As to the Farnsworth Field House, she congratulated Dr. Farnsworth "for this distinction conferred upon you" and once more asked him to thank "Mr. Bingham for the $500 check deposited in the Personal Charity fund."[394]

Early in 1938, Mrs. Hunter had attempted to assist several needy high school students in obtaining basic clothing and found herself facing overwhelming want for benevolence. Initially, she presented one of the teachers with $10 to cover the needs of several students, but soon discovered that one girl required all of the $10— and then some—to meet her basic necessities. In Mrs. Hunter's letter to Dr. Farnsworth, she asked, "Would Mr. Bingham let me help the needy students who come to my attention to make them presentable and help save their self respect?" When Will read this passage and saw Dr. Farnsworth's penciled question mark there, he wrote beside it, "by all means yes to the above."[395]

Another instance of special efforts made by Will Bingham to help individuals in need occurred following the great "1936 Flood," considered the "flood of the century," which took place in March of that year when the Androscoggin River, which passes through

Bethel and Rumford, overflowed its banks and disrupted the lives of a large number of citizens, many of whom were living on the margins.[396] Some assistance for victims came from the Red Cross, but there were a number of medical cases not handled by that agency. For example, quite a few people had lost their braces and glasses; others faced medical emergencies, such as puss-filled tonsils; and numerous farmers had to deal with the disappearance of their fences for cows. A tone of desperation characterized one of the letters Mrs. Hunter wrote to Dr. Farnsworth at this time, where she asked that he trust her to use all of the funds from Will "wisely," knowing that he might still "get me on the carpet afterward, holding over me threats of dismissal, etc."[397] It appears that no such thoughts were being considered or entertained, since Will wrote a note on the letter to Dr. Farnsworth expressing the view that "I think Mrs. H. is quite right in the way she is handling the flood money."[398]

Later, in July of that same year, Mrs. Hunter asked Dr. Farnsworth about housing for a Norwegian immigrant family in East Bethel. As things turned out, the house being investigated for possible purchase with Will's assistance was owned by a farmer whose wife was concerned that the potential buyer was an alleged imbiber of alcohol; to make the situation clear, Mrs. Hunter commented, "They don't want a drinking man in the neighborhood." That conclusion appeared to stymie any further action on the case.[399]

Both Will Bingham and George Farnsworth experienced periods during their long association when one or the other of them were besieged with serious illness. In Dr. Farnsworth's case, he suffered from a number of physical maladies that were treated by a variety of physicians; but in Will's situation, the trouble was most often psychological in nature and only required time for him to re-cover from certain debilitating mental states. In a 1936 note to George Farnsworth after the Doctor had undergone a medical procedure, Will wrote, "I hear you are getting along well, which is the best of news." He also reassured the Doctor that he himself "was decidedly better" and "not to worry about anything." Two years later, Dr. Farnsworth reported to a correspondent that Will "was not doing any business this summer, as he is recovering from a recent ill turn." This, of course, was a recurring state of affairs that doctors Gehring and Farnsworth (and, eventually, Walters) would encounter during their years of dealing with Will Bingham's varying moods and inclinations.

Another individual who served Will Bingham well for many years as his local "eyes and ears" was Betty Burns Thurston, who died in 1959. She was the second wife of Guy L. Thurston (1865-1952), who earlier oversaw logging crews in the Bethel area, operated a hardware store, and served as road commissioner and postmaster, but who, for the last twenty years of his life, worked as superintendent of the grounds, gardens, and woods of the Bethel Inn.[400] Mrs. Thurston was a professional nurse who had red hair, was of slight stature, and who kept her age a closely-guarded secret. From her obituary, it can be established that "for fifty years she gave her best to the people of Bethel," sharing "the responsibility of the rich and the problems of the poor."[401] Known for her "wise counsel" and "suggestions," she enjoyed the confidence of medical professionals and appeared to have an innate ability to anticipate their wishes.[402] She consistently set high standards, although her obituary noted that "no menial task was beneath her."[403]

One of Betty Burns Thurston's greatest "fans" was Dr. George Farnsworth, who called her his "official investigator," who "occasionally looks into some matters for me," and "pays out small sums approved by Mr. Bingham to save me the trouble of small monthly checks."[404] Farnsworth claimed that it did not matter to him if Mrs. Thurston's role as "official investigator" for him "got around," and boasted that he could not imagine "a better smoke screen for me to hide behind from time to time."[405] He even went so far in his enthusiasm for Mrs. Thurston's briefings to praise their thoroughness; if challenged, however, he contended that he had to disavow any knowledge of particular cases, declaring, "deny, I must and shall continue to do."[406]

Dr. Farnsworth held her in especially high regard and depended upon her guidance and advice in determining the merits of numerous local appeals for financial assistance from Will.[407] Mrs. Thurston had once played a leading role in managing the household staff of Dr. Farnsworth's mother, Marian, and her second husband, Dr. Gehring, so it was a seamless transition to her role as trusted assistant to Will, Dr. Farnsworth, and, later, Dr. Arthur Walters.

On at least one occasion, Mrs. Thurston and June Hills Hunter worked together to solve a quandary involving a refugee who had suffered a heart attack on a bus and was dropped off at the Bethel Inn. Notified by the Inn, Mrs. Thurston, in consultation with Bethel physician Dr. Willard Boynton, shipped the refugee to the Rumford Hospital, where he came to Mrs. Hunter's attention. She advised Dr. Farnsworth that the man had a brother in New York. In retrospect, Mrs. Thurston performed, in Dr. Farnsworth's words, "nicely" in her handling of this potentially difficult situation.[408]

As enthusiastic as Dr. Farnsworth was with Betty Thurston's service to "Mr. Bingham," her domestic life had its complications and, as will be seen, must have caused him some concern. Her stepchildren, Guy Thurston, Jr., and his sister, Bertha Thurston Charick, contested their father's will in 1952, charging that Elizabeth Burns Thurston had employed "undue influence and duress," causing their father "to separate from his first wife [their mother]."[409] In addition, according to their complaint, their father had become engaged to Lillian Dinsmore in an effort to escape Betty's influence. When Betty learned of this engagement she "threatened to bring action for breech [sic] of promise of marriage unless he ended the engagement."[410] Through "her wiles, undue influence and control over him," she "got her way," which was followed by Lillian Dinsmore's action against Guy Thurston, Sr., resulting in "heavy damages."[411] Through her "threats, persuasion and undue influence," Betty managed to marry Mr. Thurston and, "ever since, has controlled him through undue influence, wiles and domineering tactics."[412] As a consequence of her position with William Bingham 2nd as his "confidential secretary," the charges continued, she obtained for "Guy L. Thurston a position of superintendent of the grounds of some of the property [the Bethel Inn] of William Bingham II."[413] Once they were married, she "controlled their home" and through "her undue influence and control" over her husband, she prevented his making the bequests to his children that were "promised."[414] Despite these serious accusations, indications are that the step-children's complaint was never acted upon.

An event in the mid-1930s that would have wider implications for Will was a fire on February 18, 1935, in a remote part of Maine that destroyed the high school in the Aroostook County town of Hodgdon. Since the estimated population of Hodgdon at the time was only 1070, there was considerable concern in the town as to how the building could be replaced. It is not known by what means Will Bingham heard about this great misfortune, but somehow Hodgdon Superintendent of Schools D. Herman Corson prevailed upon Will to provide $60,000 toward the $102,000 necessary for the construction of the present building, which is still in use. The town and the federal government also helped, but it was Will Bingham's generous gift that made the difference in moving the project forward expeditiously. Regrettably, Will's involvement at Hodgdon soon brought requests from educational facilities all over Maine seeking his financial assistance in meeting school building needs. In response to these pleas, Dr. Farnsworth vigorously defended the notion that Will lacked the funds for additional construction projects. Farnsworth even used the example of Hodgdon to deny charity cases in the area, since, as he stated, Will's gift for that high school would "have to suffice for your section of the country for some time."[415] The Doctor urged one correspondent to "please understand that it is not because Mr. Bingham is not <u>willing</u> but he is not able," adding that "he has just so much money to give each year and when it is gone, there simply isn't any more."[416] To one inquiry for money to assist schools in Oakland, Maine, Dr. Farnsworth stressed that he had to bear the brunt of writing discouraging replies to school officials, and that "the taxers have had their way and the cow is milked dry."[417]

Another example of increased interest in school construction projects that resulted from Will's generosity in Hodgdon is documented by a written response in 1938 from Dr. Farnsworth to an inquiry from the principal of Canton High School in Canton, Maine. Farnsworth noted that the principal's letter "presents your case very appealingly, and I know you have been led to indulge in hopes from Mr. Bingham's generosity last year to certain school districts."[418] The Doctor indicated, however, that this prior benevolence was "sporadic, beyond the budget, and cannot be repeated."[419] In addition, he continued, "For what poor comfort it may give you, I must tell you that Mr. Bingham has been obliged to refuse a dozen such requests as yours and will continue to do so."[420] The Doctor declared that the main reason was "the tremendous jump in income taxes," emphasizing that the "people cannot have it both ways; they cannot tax and also receive philanthropic handouts."[421]

Perhaps no person connected with an academic institution seeking Will Bingham's financial support aroused Dr. Farnsworth's ire more fully than Lindsay Lord, Dean of Portland Junior Technical College in Maine's largest city. Citing the fact that Will had written on Lord's letter "no contribution," Farnsworth continued, "I must assume (from experience) that your letter is intended to be an opening wedge; therefore, I shall put you out of your misery at once."[422] His hostile tone persisted, "Under no circumstances will Mr. Bingham be able to add to his educational budget" as "I have this in his own handwriting on your letter, with request to transmit it to you."[423] From there Farnsworth went on to assure Dean Lord of his interest in and sympathy for youth, but closed with his frequently recited diatribe against the "Share the

William Bingham 2nd at about age 6
(Gould Academy Archives, Bethel Historical Society)

The three oldest Bingham children at play, Cleveland (Payne Archives)

Oliver, William, Elizabeth, Frances, and Henry Bingham (Payne Archives)

Will and Oliver Bingham reading at home (Payne Archives)

The Bingham family traveled often by private rail car (Payne Archives)

Will Bingham on horseback (Payne Archives)

Will Bingham and friend (Payne Archives)

*The Charles Bingham residence on Euclid Avenue, Cleveland
(Payne Archives)*

The Bingham family at Palm Beach, Florida (Payne Archives)

Will Bingham with a "jack" in Florida (Payne Archives)

"Figulus," the Charles Bingham estate in Florida (Payne Archives)

*The Bingham family at "Figulus"; Will Bingham second from left
(Payne Archives)*

Oliver and Will Bingham at "Figulus" (Payne Archives)

St. Paul's School, Concord, New Hampshire (Author's Collection)

Frances and Will Bingham in Colonial costume (Payne Archives)

Will Bingham, location unknown (Payne Archives)

The Gehring residence and Clinic, Bethel (Bethel Historical Society)

Drawing room at the Gehring house/Clinic (Bethel Historical Society)

Dr. John George Gehring (Bethel Historical Society)

Marian True Gehring (Bethel Historical Society)

Mary True, renowned teacher of the deaf (Bethel Historical Society)

"The Delinda," Broad Street home of Mary True (Bethel Historical Society)

"The Cathedral Elms of Broad Street" (Bethel Historical Society)

*Gehring Clinic patients; Will Bingham center, back row
(Bethel Historical Society)*

Fresh air and regular exercise was part of the Gehring Clinic "treatment"
(Bethel Historical Society)

Winter "exercise" at the Gehring Clinic; Will Bingham on right
(Bethel Historical Society)

*Will Bingham and William Upson at Gehring House
(Bethel Historical Society)*

Grand Trunk Railway station, Bethel (Bethel Historical Society)

The Bethel Inn under construction, October 1912 (Bethel Historical Society)

*Long owned by Will Bingham, the Bethel Inn opened in July 1913
(Bethel Historical Society)*

The main lobby of the Bethel Inn boasts a bronze Tiffany Company plaque honoring the work of Dr. John George Gehring (Bethel Historical Society)

Close-up of plaque above (Bethel Historical Society)

THIS INN STANDS AS A VISIBLE EXPRESSION
OF APPRECIATION OF AN UNUSUAL PHYSICIAN
AND OF GRATITUDE FOR THE INSPIRING PERSONALITY
SHOWN IN THE WORK OF
JOHN GEORGE GEHRING, M.D.
AND HAS BEEN MADE POSSIBLE
THROUGH THE RECOGNITION OF
HORACE S. SEARS, BOSTON, MASS.   ROBERT WINSOR, BOSTON, MASS.
CHARLES W. HUBBARD, BOSTON, MASS. WILLIAM H. UPSON, CLEVELAND, OHIO
WILLIAM BINGHAM, CLEVELAND, OHIO

Tally-ho coach at Bethel Inn, circa 1915 (Bethel Historical Society)

Early 20th century advertisement for the Inn (Bethel Historical Society)

Members of the "Bethel League" at the Inn; Will Bingham in back row, left (with hat); Dr. and Mrs. Gehring center back (Bethel Historical Society)

St. Valentine's Day party at Gehring Clinic, 1913; Will Bingham second from left, back row; Dr. and Mrs. Gehring at center (Bethel Historical Society)

*Will Bingham and Mrs. Charles A. Sherman of Flushing, New York,
performing for members of the Bethel League circa 1916
(Gould Academy Archives, Bethel Historical Society)*

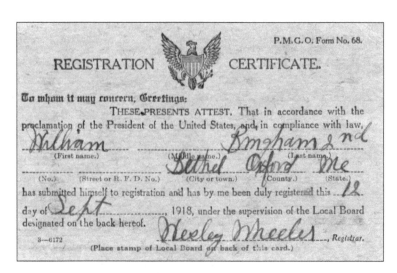

Will Bingham's World War I registration certificate
(Gould Academy Archives, Bethel Historical Society)

Bethel attorney Ellery C. Park (Bethel Historical Society)

"Mother Goose & Her Family," Gehring Clinic, March 1914
Will Bingham, second from left (Bethel Historical Society)

Oliver Hazard Payne, brother of Will Bingham's mother, died in 1917,
leaving his nieces and nephews a substantial inheritance (Payne Archives)

*Will Bingham residence on Broad Street, Bethel
(Bethel Historical Society)*

*William Bingham Gymnasium, constructed in 1921-1922 at Gould Academy
(Bethel Historical Society)*

Marian True Gehring Students' Home, 1924-1925, Gould Academy
(Bethel Historical Society)

Broad Street, Bethel, circa 1940; village common and Bethel Inn on right
(Bethel Historical Society)

Broad Street residence of William J. Upson; theater/music room on right
(Bethel Historical Society)

Will Bingham, Mr. Harp, and William J. Upson at Bethel
(Bethel Historical Society)

Memorial plaque at Robert College, Istanbul, Turkey
(Çiğdem Yazıcıoğlu, Robert College Alumni & Development Office)

West Parish Congregational Church (Bethel Historical Society)

Gray Athletic Building completed at Bates College in 1927
(Edmund S. Muskie Archives and Special Collections Library)

Rumford Community Hospital (Bethel Historical Society)

In 1933-1934, Gould Academy's 1881 classroom building was replaced by a Georgian Revival structure named for longtime principal Frank E. Hanscom (both, Bethel Historical Society)

Dr. George Bourne Farnsworth
(Gould Academy Archives, Bethel Historical Society)

"Farnstede Manor," the Farnsworth home at Damariscotta, Maine
(Gould Academy Archives, Bethel Historical Society)

*Letterhead showing locations of the "Bingham office" during
the era of Dr. George B. Farnsworth's management
(Gould Academy Archives, Bethel Historical Society)*

(Courtesy of Digital Collections and Archives, Tufts University)

Bingham plaque at Pratt Diagnostic Hospital
(Courtesy of Digital Collections and Archives, Tufts University)

Farnsworth Field House construction at Gould Academy, 1941
(Bethel Historical Society)

Farnsworth Surgical Wing of the New England Medical Center
(Courtesy of Digital Collections and Archives, Tufts University)

(Courtesy of Digital Collections and Archives, Tufts University)

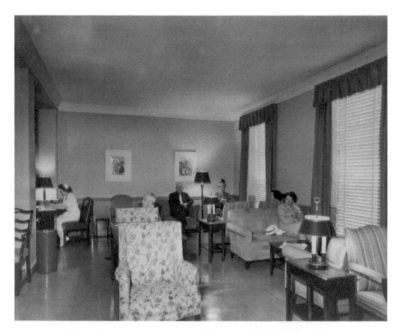

Clinic lounge at Farnsworth Surgical Building, 1949
(Courtesy of Digital Collections and Archives, Tufts University)

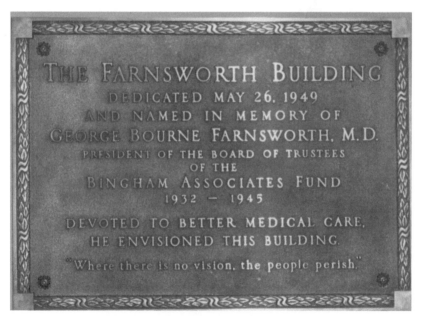

THE FARNSWORTH BUILDING
DEDICATED MAY 26, 1949
AND NAMED IN MEMORY OF
GEORGE BOURNE FARNSWORTH, M.D.
PRESIDENT OF THE BOARD OF TRUSTEES
OF THE
BINGHAM ASSOCIATES FUND
1932 — 1945

DEVOTED TO BETTER MEDICAL CARE,
HE ENVISIONED THIS BUILDING.

"Where there is no vision, the people perish."

(Courtesy of Digital Collections and Archives, Tufts University)

Dr. Arthur L. Walters
(Gould Academy Archives, Bethel Historical Society)

TO THE MEMORY OF
WILLIAM BINGHAM 2ND.
TRUSTEE 1917 – 1955
DEVOTED BENEFACTOR
– OF –
GOULD ACADEMY

Erected by the Class of 1955

Memorial plaque on the Gould Academy athletic field
(Bethel Historical Society)

PROGRAM

**DEDICATION OF
BINGHAM HALL**

October 5, 1963

GOULD ACADEMY
BETHEL   MAINE

(Gould Academy Archives, Bethel Historical Society)

Frances Payne Bolton speaking at 1963 dedication of Bingham Hall
(Bethel Historical Society)

Frances Payne Bolton, Dr. Sidney Davidson, and Dr. Samuel Proger, 1963
(Bethel Historical Society)

William Bingham 2nd, philanthropist and benefactor

William Bingham's gravestone at Cleveland's Lake View Cemetery
(Author's Collection)

Wealth" philosophy of the government and its alleged hostility to those with philanthropic inclinations.

In the midst of all this philanthropic oversight, Dr. Farnsworth's mother's death in December 1936 made it necessary for her only child to settle her estate. In a letter to his Uncle Bert, Farnsworth expressed the sentiment that "an era came to an end."[424] He recalled with some nostalgic sentiment the house and barn of his grandfather's era that burned in 1896 to be replaced by "that bastard erection of 1896 which I have thankfully passed on."[425] The purchaser turned out to be none other than the quiet man who lived next door—Will Bingham. The contents of the house, characterized by Dr. Farnsworth as "four van loads of very, very 2nd hand furniture," were shipped to his "fisherman's cottages" at Christmas Cove, Maine, which he bought "for protection" and which he was transforming into "Lendy Houses," as he described them, "for my dear but often less fortunate friends."[426]

It is interesting to note at this juncture that not all of Will's educational efforts resulted in success. One of the sorriest examples of misplaced Bingham support for college attendance during Dr. Farnsworth's tenure was the case of a Gould graduate who came from a large local family. Even Headmaster Elwood Ireland was economical in his January 1943 letter of recommendation, noting that she was "a country girl" and "of average ability," but with "plenty of vitality and personality to make a good teacher."[427] He expressed the opinion that she "can undoubtedly do the normal school work" and would not be able to go beyond Gould without financial assistance.[428] She received a loan of $300 from Will Bingham and went off to a Maine normal school with the goal of becoming a home economics teacher.

It was not until after the end of the first semester that a normal school official reported to Dr. Farnsworth that the freshman was not one of their high ranking students, having come there with poor study habits and Gould Academy marks that were lower than those of students they ordinarily accepted.[429] One can only imagine how distraught Dr. Farnsworth must have been upon reading in the report that her grades were all D's, except for C's in Physical Education and English. Farnsworth immediately contacted her, declaring that of all the students he had been associated with regarding Bingham scholarships, no one had ever presented such low grades. He informed her that significant growth had to be achieved in the second semester in order for her to continue her education. The student responded to this warning by implausibly reminding the Doctor that a grade of "C" was considered "very good rank here," and promised to work conscientiously in the second semester.[430]

Despite these assurances, it's evident that not much changed over the following semester, since the same normal school official informed Dr. Farnsworth that the student had been unable to pass some of her courses. Consequently, the school spokesperson recommended she attend a fashion retailing "school," even though, as he stated, "her prospects are dim."[431] Subsequently, the student followed up on the suggestion that she explore fashion retailing, but, once again, the account of her performance forwarded to Dr. Farnsworth was not encouraging. In this no-nonsense report, one of the fashion officials declared that the potential student was "plump, pink and white and very, very vague, and her only reason for wanting to get into retailing I judge is that she thinks she has a flair for clothes."[432] The executive continued, "I suppose that is the worst reason in the world for undertaking this type of career."[433] In fact, the fashion maven wrote, she is "a type all too common who does not know very much but never discovers the fact." In closing, she added, "I would say she had a rather pudgy mind and the bland expression that indicates a tranquil disposition and complete paucity of ideas."[434]

In response to this extremely unfavorable report, Dr. Farnsworth wrote to the failing student that it was "preposterous to think of advancing you the required amount for the Chamberlain

School."[435] In addition, he underscored the fact that Mr. Bingham "never gives grants to non-collegiate institutions [as in the case of the Chamberlain School] which are run for profit."[436] He urged her to accept whatever job offers came along, "and discover any talents if any you may have."[437] To the fashion retailer, Dr. Farnsworth was especially blunt, insisting that Bingham scholarships could not be wasted on "dumbbells."[438] The student, he proclaimed, "should go to work as soon as possible," adding that he hated to "blight a young person," but in this case he knew the retailer agreed with him.[439] This same sentiment had been expressed in an earlier letter to the normal school dean, where Dr. Farnsworth wrote that the failing student clearly could not "make the grade," noting that it was not her fault "that her brain does not function on the academic level."[440]

Dr. Farnsworth was involved in at least one other instance of closely reviewing and evaluating a student's academic performance in connection with Will Bingham's support. In 1939, two Gould Academy graduates attending Russell Sage College in Troy, New York, were reported by the president of that institution, Dr. Helen McInstry, to have received passing, but low marks. The offending students received letters from Dr. Farnsworth chastising them and noting that this level of performance was not a strong argument for future scholarships. In his letter to President Helen McInstry, Farnsworth wrote, "[it is] not our custom to underwrite mediocre material, and I am pained and shocked at your preliminary report of C and D grades."[441] He continued in the letter to express his outrage at this state of affairs, particularly citing his "interest because of William Bingham" and his position "as President of the Gould Academy Board of Trustees."[442] In regard to the latter, he pledged to "investigate any suspicion of inadequacy" on the part of the Academy.[443]

Of course, not all of Dr. Farnsworth's relationships with Bingham scholarship students were so adversarial, and some situations actually made him appear to be a "genial uncle." Such was the case of Virginia Louise Brown of Gorham, Maine, who sent Will Bingham a recording of her singing and whom Farnsworth believed to be a talented musical student. Dr. Farnsworth acknowledged the arrival of the record to Brown, promising it would be played for Will on his "super duper phonograph."[444] In a later letter to Miss Brown, Dr. Farnsworth confided that he was glad to leave the practice of surgery where "everyone was a number" and he was a "body carpenter."[445] He rejoiced in his current role, working with a philanthropist making educational grants to students that have "a most delightful way of keeping me in touch with their lives and thereby my own is greatly enriched."[446] He even invited Miss Brown to visit him at Christmas Cove, and assured her that he would bring her scholarship information to the attention of Mr. Bingham, "who is a great music lover and who for many years played the violin."[447]

Another student, Betty Price, who was the recipient of Bingham scholarship assistance to attend the University of Maine, and later became a doctor, received instructions from Dr. Farnsworth to write him anything, good or bad, as he served as "father confessor" to "my student grant youngsters."[448] He even related the story that, when he was in his first year at Harvard Medical School, he hired "a colored maid" to clean his apartment.[449] While dusting behind some curtains, the maid discovered a human skeleton and screeched in fright. The event caused quite a scene, according to Farnsworth, as he had to explain the presence of a skeleton to the police. In a later letter, Dr. Farnsworth confided to Miss Price the means by which, as a student, he had sometimes overcome adversity: "I used to hop a steamer out of Boston to Europe and let the sea blow away my troubles."[450]

Another student beneficiary of Will Bingham's philanthropic outlays was Dr. Farnsworth's uncle's grandson, Nathaniel True Bartholomaei, a descendant (and namesake) of Bethel's celebrated educator and historian, Dr. Nathaniel Tuckerman True. Bartholomaei was born with an eye that required surgery, arranged for by Dr. Farnsworth and funded by Will Bingham. "Nat" Bartholomaei graduated from Gould Academy in 1940 and was accepted at the University of Maine to study engineering.[451]

Predictably, Dr. Farnsworth was full of advice for his young cousin as he advanced his first $400 Bingham scholarship. He described Nat's opportunity for a Maine education as his "great chance," and in his best fatherly manner advised him not to "muff it or play the giddy goad because we crack down relentlessly on all grantees who do."[452] He warned his cousin that scholarship recipients "get no second chance" since "we have more than we can handle, so the no-goods go out on their ears."[453] As a True descendant, he had to live up to high standards, according to the Doctor, since "many a man has missed honors at the end of his college course because of stupidity, irresponsibility, bewilderment and lack of application THE FIRST SEMESTER!"[454] He urged Nat to stay in communication with his office, and "hop to it, have the time of your life in vigorous, normal ways and justify your own existence and our pride in you."[455]

To Natalie True Bartholomaei (1900-2002), his first cousin and Nat's mother, Dr. Farnsworth wrote that scholarship recipients such as Nat should receive "the highest marks the boy is capable of" and warned her that those receiving assistance from Will were required to have "perfect behavior" and observe "strict economy."[456] He warned that "no excuses are accepted for stupidity, waste and extravagance," and any violation meant grants "merely stop."[457] The Doctor then requested that "Than" [Nat] read his letter to her "carefully," adding that, since "he is a little older than most freshmen, I shall expect more of him."[458]

Nat Bartholomaei did well at the University of Maine and enjoyed a successful engineering career. Dr. Farnsworth was amused when a woman Nat was dating during his years at the University appealed to him to convey to his cousin that although she liked Nat, she was not in love and wanted to break up with him and urge him

to date other girls.[459] Dr. Farnsworth, in a letter to the woman involved, expressed amusement with his "anti-Cupid" role, and in a
communication to Nat urged him to know as many women as
possible.[460]

Some Bingham scholarship applicants were denied support
when it could be established that they had sufficient family
monetary backing. Dr. Farnsworth relied on at least two local
sources—Betty Burns Thurston and Bethel attorney Ellery C.
Park—to ascertain the financial status of certain applicants for
assistance. They played influential roles in directing Will's
philanthropy in the Bethel area, since he wanted to help as many
needy students as possible. In one instance, Ellery Park wrote to
Dr. Farnsworth, commenting that a certain request "surprises me."
He continued on with the opinion that this family should be able to
pay for their daughter's business education. The case was referred
to Will, who asked Neal Dale (Farnsworth's son-in-law) to
investigate further. Evidently, Will was not happy to learn that the
father of this student had been found "loafing on the Bethel Inn's
nickel," so the painting job he had been hired to do was withdrawn
from him. Will also suggested that the applicant "wait a year and
see what develops."[461]

A similar case in which Bethel attorney Ellery Park provided
input was a request from a mother for her son's support, even
though he lived with her and could work. Since mother and son
were related to a prominent and prosperous Bethel figure, Dr.
Farnsworth, in his response to the mother, questioned why the son
did not work and why she did not apply to her relative, as "it would
be more fitting for you to apply to him [rather] than a stranger."[462]

When another young man from Mexico, Maine, requested
assistance, Dr. Farnsworth urged him to go into the military, acquire
a skill there, and secure a good retirement. If he learned a fine trade
elsewhere, Farnsworth assured him, he would "have seen
something better than the back yards of Rumford."[463] The Doctor
continued in a similar manner, alleging that "not many Maine boys

have the ability or guts" to continue working. None such should expect any assistance under his "watch," since, he emphasized, "Mr. Bingham's philanthropic expenditures are budgeted years ahead, and in general are applied only to physical relief and illness," and "the occasional exception often represents an experiment not likely to be repeated."[464]

Yet another case, this one discovered by June Hills Hunter in the course of her tuberculosis work in the Rumford area, involved a young man, Robert Chandler, of Ridlonville, a section of Mexico, Maine, bordering on Rumford; according to Hunter, Chandler's face was badly "scarred" with acne.[465] He was a Mexico High School graduate who had attended the flagship campus of the University of Maine at Orono for one semester, became discouraged, and left the University. He inquired of Mrs. Hunter to see if he could go to Maine Central Institute in Pittsfield, and then back to the University of Maine to study chemistry, mathematics, and engineering. In her letter to Dr. Farnsworth, she considered Chandler's case "more worthwhile and hopeful" than others in the area.[466] She explained that he had been willed a house, which might be sold to assist in funding his education, and was assigned a guardian, since he was a minor. He had tried to enter the military, but was rejected for reasons not known. She suggested to Dr. Farnsworth that Chandler's case might be a good one for Will to take on.

Earlier correspondence reveals that Will had already notified Dr. Farnsworth of his willingness to send "Bob" Chandler to Dr. Pratt in Boston for treatment of his badly disfigured face.[467] If Dr. Pratt was unable to help him, Will offered to refer Chandler to Dr. Pels in Baltimore as a Bingham case. He noted with approval that Chandler was a "protégé" of Deputy Sheriff John Johnson in Mexico, and that Mrs. Thurston or Mrs. Hunter could oversee his trip to Baltimore. Surviving correspondence does not reveal what happened to Chandler in regard to his facial disfigurement, but he did return to the University of Maine. Dr. Farnsworth thanked Deputy Sheriff Johnson for supplying Chandler's grades, at the same time warning that Chandler's marks in algebra were "too low for an intending scientist." Farnsworth also shared his often repeated belief that "Maine grades are ten percent higher than those in Massachusetts and New York," which he believed was a result of more relaxed grading standards in the Pine Tree State.[468] In reaction to this perceived disparity, the Doctor reiterated one of his favorite maxims, directing Maine students "to stretch their minds and increase their abilities before tackling higher education."[469] It appears that Bob Chandler received another opportunity to attend the University of Maine, since he received a check from Will for $580 along with an admonition from Dr. Farnsworth reminding him that "you have been there before" and "you are not likely to play giddy goat like some Freshman."[470] The Doctor also urged him to "use my name" and to befriend Percy Crane, the University of Maine's Director of Admissions and a former Gould Academy assistant Headmaster, who "has been helpful to many of our boys and girls."[471]

One other student from the Rumford area contacted Dr. Farnsworth, requesting $1000 to attend Harvard University. The Doctor responded by advising him that educational grants were usually limited to $500 annually. He advised the student to select a Maine college, since it was likely to be "less expensive."[472]

Among the "rules" that Dr. Farnsworth insisted upon in order to receive a Bingham scholarship was that boys should work in the summer. One recipient, Daniel F. Hanley, who served as a lifeguard in the summer of 1933 at Salisbury Beach, Massachusetts, recalled (and recorded in December 1997) his experiences with Dr. Farnsworth in considerable detail:

> Labor Day Weekend of 1933, I was a lifeguard at Salisbury Beach, Mass. when I received a telegram from Dr. Farnsworth (of the Bingham Fund) telling me to be at his house at Christmas Cove, Maine the next morning. He had received my name from Dean Nixon of Bowdoin College. Dean Nixon, in a letter, had

told him that I had been admitted to Medical School and had graduated from Bowdoin with a good record and also that I was broke. My family and I were without a car so I went to the Ford Dealer in Amesbury and asked if I could borrow a car for a day. He loaned me a car and filled it with gas. The next morning my sister Connie and I got a map of Maine and took off for Christmas Cove. At that time the bridge in Bath was a toll bridge. We had enough money between us to get over and back. We drove to the Christmas Cove Hotel and asked the man at the desk to use the telephone to call Dr. Farnsworth. He said Dr. Farnsworth lived close by. I called and told him I was at the hotel and received directions to his house.

Arriving at the house, I knocked and was met by a girl who asked me in and told me to sit down and wait. I sat for about twenty minutes during which time, a man in a bathrobe, a beret and a long cigarette holder walked by me three or four times before entering a room close by.

The lady who had admitted me to the house announced I could now see Dr. Farnsworth. She took me in and introduced me. He started right off telling me he didn't give scholarships to people who stayed at the hotel. I told him I didn't stay there but merely stopped to telephone. He told me they didn't give scholarships to boys who have cars. I told him I didn't have a car, but had borrowed it from a dealer. He then asked me what medical school I was going to. I told him Columbia in New York City. He then made a face and with a look of disgust said, "They are all Jews and Catholics there." I said nothing. Then he said Dean Nixon of Bowdoin had written a good reference letter and Mr. Bingham wants to give you a scholarship but "I'm against it, but Mr. Bingham is the boss!" He took a check out of a drawer and handed it to me, one thousand dollars (more money than I had seen in my life). He told me he would call me in New York every year in the fall and the spring and that I should come to his location and report to him. I thanked him for the check and his interest and left.

Each year for four years while at Columbia Medical School, in the spring and fall, I would receive a letter from Dr.

Farnsworth giving me his telephone number and location in the city. The letters were always in Capitals and addressed in Capital letters. I would phone him and after giving my name he would say, "Who the hell are you?" I would say "I'm calling to report, when do you want to see me" He often said, "Don't they have any classes at that medical school? He then would give me [an] appointment at seven o'clock the next morning. I would be at his hotel at 7 a.m. His secretary would be working at a typewriter. She would tell me to sit and wait. Dr. Farnsworth would be in his bathrobe, beret and puffing his cigarette in a long cigarette holder. He would pass me two or three times then admit me to his office. On one occasion upon entering, he told me, "You're too fat." With each visit this episode was often repeated. On my last visit in the spring of 1939, Dr. Farnsworth told me Mr. Bingham had cancelled all debt and that I owed him nothing. I thanked him and asked if I could see Mr. Bingham. He told me that "No one sees Mr. Bingham," so I asked him to convey my thanks when he saw him.

Having graduated from Columbia [1943], I was soon in the Army in India, Burma, and China. In northern Burma, I bought a long carved ivory cigarette holder for Dr. Farnsworth. I carried it through Burma and China and on to Germany when I took the "Nazi Party of the Orient" back to Germany. I finally came home with the cigarette holder in 1946 only to find that Dr. Farnsworth had passed away [Farnsworth actually died the following May 1947].

In appreciation and thanks for Dr. Farnsworth and Mr. Bingham's help though medical school, I established a scholarship in Dr. Farnsworth's name at Bowdoin College and donated the cigarette holder to the Bethel Historical Society.[473]

Dr. Hanley, as noted above, was not intimidated by Dr. Farnsworth's brusque treatment during his medical school days. He took it in stride and with good humor, establishing, as he referenced in his brief memoir, a Farnsworth Scholarship at his beloved

Bowdoin, where he served as college physician for thirty-three years.

In a pattern that remained constant throughout the Farnsworth-Bingham years, two sisters who received Bingham assistance in obtaining their higher education also received admonitions from Dr. Farnsworth. The younger sister, a Gould Academy graduate, was counseled to "justify the education you have received."[474] When her scholarship check arrived, the Doctor advised her to immediately place it in the bank and to "guard it well," for "it must last you."[475] Earlier, her older sister had received $250 from Will Bingham to attend the Maine School of Commerce in Auburn. In this case, Dr. Farnsworth affirmed that Bingham funds usually were not expended for "business educations," but, in this case, an exception was being made since, as he acknowledged to the recipient, she was "a Bethel girl" and "a G.A. graduate," as well as "one of this generation of [Bethel] Cloughs and Carters."[476] Dr. Farnsworth urged her to keep this exception confidential and to work hard to be in the upper half of her class so that she would be in a position to land a position after graduation.

Another Bingham scholarship recipient, who Farnsworth described as "relatively young and inexperienced," induced the Doctor to request that Elizabeth Melville, Dean of Westbrook College in Portland, look after the student's finances. In his letter to the Dean, Farnsworth also seized upon the opportunity to boast about the fine state of the educational facilities at Gould Academy and its more than a century of existence. He particularly pointed out that the Bethel school had the "largest physical equipment and endowment of any academy in Maine for which I have built over a million dollars of new buildings in the last six years."[477] Absent from this statement, of course, was any reference to William Bingham 2nd, who had provided *all* of the funding for the buildings at Gould Academy, for which the Doctor was brazenly taking credit.

Beyond all this concern for the worthiness of scholarship students, there arose occasionally other beneficiaries of Will Bingham's largesse who, not being held in high esteem by Dr. Farnsworth, directly or indirectly received the sharp edge of his tongue. One example was a woman who was treated by Dr. Proger, at Will's request, through the efforts of his nurse, Eva Boggs, who pitied the individual and influenced her boss to assist the lady. Dr. Farnsworth contemptuously referred to her, without stating why, as "a bit of flotsam."[478] He insisted that there was no reason for Will to support her except for a "broad charitable humanitarian viewpoint," and no reason why this "bit of human wreckage should receive a degree of support unwarranted by any claim of just desserts."[479]

In another instance, Dr. Farnsworth was particularly harsh in dismissing a request by a Bethel woman who had once worked at the Bethel Inn. He reminded her that William Bingham was "flooded with such appeals as yours, so has to limit [them] to those absolutely helpless."[480] He urged her to realize that Will faced loss of income and increased taxation. He also pointed out that she had only worked briefly for the Bethel Inn and that "was long ago and the circumstances do not entitle you to special consideration."[481] In Farnsworth's defense, it seems that Betty Burns Thurston had investigated this case and provided Dr. Farnsworth with information confirming that the woman was receiving income from the rent of her farm, had no dependents, and could mortgage her property to provide herself with "ready cash."[482] Farnsworth therefore urged her to go to the county and town for relief.

Another example of Dr. Farnsworth's bluntness was his response in 1941 to a newly arrived Bethel physician, Harry Wilson, who was complaining that he was receiving a decidedly cold, if not hostile, reception from the other Bethel medical professionals, and had not been chosen to fill a position funded by Will Bingham. "Cheer up," Farnsworth advised, "Everyone who has ever tried to help a rural community has been crucified, including Dr. Gehring in 1890 and Jesus Christ in the year 32."[483] In addition, Farnsworth also pointedly reminded Dr. Wilson that Will and he "already have our man picked for this job."[484] What was more, Dr. Farnsworth expressed the sentiment that he was "sorry" that Dr. Wilson "could not have qualified for it," but cited the instance "when I tried to start you on an educational program, when you first came to town which might easily have led to such a position, [but] you turned me down flat."[485] To this statement Farnsworth added, "Of course I realize that it was from ignorance and a very limited experience and vision, and I never held it against you, but was sorry that you did not recognize the opportunity."[486] He continued on with his rebuke, observing that "this blindness affects the careers of so many men with whom I have come in contact in my varied life."[487] Dr. Farnsworth closed his letter by praising Dr. Wilson for trying to do his duty in "such undeveloped surroundings," citing his memory of fifty years before, hearing someone utter at a local town meeting, "What's good enough for my father is good enough for my son."[488]

In at least one case, Dr. Farnsworth's candor in denying a request for funds was considered by Will to be too brusque. In an undated letter (possibly written around 1938) to Dr. Lawrence W. Baker who was seeking financial support for his institution, Dr. Farnsworth wrote, "it seems only fair to you, that you should know that Mr. Bingham has not the slightest intention of making any contribution to the Dental School."[489] "He is not against the cause," Dr. Farnsworth assured him, but "it is simply and solely because he is committed to a line of philanthropic work that takes and will take all his available funds for years to come."[490] Farnsworth concluded his remarks by noting, "It will save you much grief if you will realize this fact, and enable you to concentrate upon more productive fields."[491] A hand-written note by Will on this letter relayed his reaction: "If you would alter this a bit, o.k.," followed by, "Need not return to me for approval. W.B."[492] Gently admonished by the great philanthropist, Dr. Farnsworth no doubt softened his response, but to what degree is unknown.

One other instance where Will urged Dr. Farnsworth to respond "tactfully" dealt with receipt of a book, *The Mind That Found Itself*, by Clifford Beers. Will described it as "interesting and a big field, but not for me, I think, at least at present."[493] Praised by famed psychologist William James, the book deals with the author's often brutal experience with mental illness in several institutions; having recovered, he became a crusader for mental health through the National Committee for Mental Hygiene and other allied organizations. Will's inclination to resist the book in light of its subject is, perhaps, not surprising. To Dr. Farnsworth, Beers was "an interesting cuss" who wanted money to publish more of his books, expended lots of cash on his book projects, and, in the Doctor's judgment, appeared weak in management skills.[494]

In February 1939, Dr. Farnsworth had serious surgery to remove his prostate. During the three months of his post-operative recovery, he continued to work out of his bed. As he wrote one correspondent, he was proud that the "office never shut down" and was "running" 200 letters per week.[495]

It was during the 1930s that Will Bingham began a gradual withdrawal of financial support for significant Cleveland institutions. In the 1920s, following World War I, he had been quite generous to many Cleveland causes. But, by the mid-1930s, he rarely visited his home town and had only limited contact with relatives and friends there. In 1937, he asked Dr. Farnsworth to decline "tactfully" any further contributions to the Cleveland Museum of Art, an institution that his father had played an instrumental role in founding.[496] In addition, Will instructed Dr. Farnsworth in 1939 to refuse requests for any funds to upgrade the Bingham Laboratory of Mechanical Engineering at the Case School of Applied Science, built in 1926-27 in Cleveland with a $500,000 gift from Will's father that was matched by Will with an equal sum for endowment.[497] It is worth noting that Will had conferred with his siblings and, in a note on this letter, declared that "they have not the money available and cannot do anything."[498]

Even though Will eventually reduced his contributions to the Cleveland Community Chest, he was always very proud of its good work. In 1936 he informed Dr. Farnsworth that, if possible, he was inclined to give them $20,000 since, in his words, there "is not a better place to invest funds in philanthropic undertakings."[499] One much later gift to a Cleveland institution facilitated by Will's last personal physician, Dr. Walters, should also be mentioned because it occurred in 1951 and amounted to $10,000 for the benefit of the Psychiatric Department of Western Reserve School of Medicine.[500]

Frequently during his tenure as Will's advisor, Dr. Farnsworth assumed the role of fiscal restrainer on Bingham's philanthropic enthusiasm and endeavors. For instance, when Will was inclined to provide $4000 to an Interseminary Commission for Training for the Rural Ministry in honor of their good work, Farnsworth did not disagree with the cause, but stated, "you are not to bear the burden," pointing out that this Commission depended "too much on one contribution."[501] In his judgment, $4000 was "too great a proportion" of the $10,000 goal.[502] He urged a $500 gift as being "more than ample."[503]

In another instance, this one also involving a religious entity—The Oxford County United Parish—in 1942, Dr. Farnsworth assured Will that the organization could get along without any contribution. Nevertheless, Will was strongly in favor of a $1000 donation, and instructed Dr. Farnsworth to send them that amount, stating, "I am sure they can make good use of it."[504] Dr. Farnsworth had earlier taken it upon himself to deny the group any funds and wondered why there was no reaction to his negative response. Will's understanding of this lack of a reply was plausibly stated: "They didn't write in but I believe having in mind the large total given to the Parish over the years, they felt timid about doing so and just didn't."[505] In any case, Will prevailed with his $1000 gift.

By the 1940s, with increasingly higher taxes consuming potential philanthropic funds, Will's focus appeared to be more and more on Maine charities. An indication of this direction was his announced reduction of contributions to the Community Chest of Dade County, Florida, so that he could provide more funds for good causes in the Pine Tree State, such as the T.B. Sanitarium in Hebron that, in Will's words, was "one of the best in Maine."[506]

Every so often, a financial plea to rescue a floundering church typically brought forth quite a "sermon" from Dr. Farnsworth. In an October 1937 letter to Haywood Burton, Treasurer of a Portsmouth, New Hampshire, church, he assured Mr. Burton that he "would not have you think we are unmindful of or unsympathetic with the struggles of the small church," but "unfortunately, however, it has been our experience that when a local church in a community is no longer able to support itself and its Pastor by its own efforts, it is already on the road to extinction."[507] He continued in his typical frank manner on this subject by stating that "the end is near when a church becomes a parasite and can only continue its existence with outside help" and "has therefore passed its period of usefulness in the community."[508] It was, in the Doctor's opinion, "better to close it and send the members to a going church," since in the present day "dogma and theology are of so little importance that it really makes little difference what church one attends, provided it be a church in active service."[509] Something close to this text was used repeatedly for many inquiries Will Bingham received from religious institutions. For instance, to a request for assistance for the Bethel Methodist Church, Dr. Farnsworth, again rejecting any creedal differences, declared, "Mr. Bingham and I feel very strongly that the hope of religious life in Bethel lies in Union, in the strength and power of Union."[510] To underscore his point that religious differences were minimal, the Doctor outlined his own personal spiritual evolution, citing his beginning as "a Boston Unitarian," and from there "a Boston Congregationalist," then "a Cleveland Presbyterian," and, finally, his attendance at an "Easter Service in an Episcopal Chapel."[511] Notwithstanding Farnsworth's opinion and "despite misgivings" of his own, Will instructed Farnsworth to send the Bethel church $100.[512]

In at least one instance of denying a church's request, both Dr. Farnsworth and Will appeared clearly sympathetic. The plea came from former Maine Republican and U.S. Congressman Donald Partridge of Norway, on behalf of the Second Congregational Church of that community, which is located about 20 miles south of Bethel. From Dr. Farnsworth, the former congressman received the "Sharing the Wealth" diatribe where, in the Doctor's words, "private and highly intelligent philanthropy is extinguished in favor of destructive taxation"; Farnsworth then concluded by saying they had to deny their request "with genuine regret."[513] Even Will, in a personally hand-written note, expressed his disquieting decision of having to "regretfully decline" assistance, citing his "concentration on medical and related causes with a few educational commitments, etc."[514]

The fact that Partridge had served as a member of Congress may have prompted the rather compassionate treatment he received. However, when the current congressman in 1939, James C. Oliver (also a Republican who later was elected as a Democrat), requested an interview with Will Bingham, he aroused Dr. Farnsworth's suspicion of a "Touch" and was curtly dismissed with the humorous notion of the Doctor's "pleasure to grant interviews with myself, since Mr. Bingham does not personally give interviews for any purpose."[515]

Another exception in providing assistance to needy churches was a second gift of $100 to the Bethel Methodist Church made at Dr. Farnsworth's own initiative, as Will was at that time unable to discuss any business, which was sometimes the case. Speaking for his superior, Farnsworth assured the requester that this donation was being made "with the distinct understanding" that "Mr. Bingham will be entirely at liberty to deny any further request in later years."[516] Dr. Farnsworth provided this contribution with a reminder to the recipient of a previous outlay, and the assertion that he (Farnsworth) was "not at all sure that it was his [Will's] intention to ever repeat it."[517]

A special example of Will's generosity toward a religious body is the $5000 he donated in 1937 to the Bethel Congregational

Church to upgrade the interior and paint the exterior once the steeple (removed in 1899 because of its deteriorated condition) was replaced under the supervision of the noted Maine architect John Calvin Stevens of Portland.[518]

Sometimes when no other avenue appeared available to deny scholarship assistance, Dr. Farnsworth used geography as an excuse. However, even in light of the preference for Maine residents, which Farnsworth repeatedly emphasized in outlining the Bingham philanthropic priorities, particular students from all over the nation received assistance in some form or another. Admittedly their numbers were not large, but it did happen, this despite Dr. Farnsworth's denial of a medical scholarship for a student from Boston because his location was deemed "outside of our geographic limits."[519]

Another strategy employed by Dr. Farnsworth in denying Bingham support was to announce boldly to the potential applicant that he was aware of the purpose of their visit or reason for contacting him. For example, to Dr. Edward Hume, who sent him a report and a collection of photos about his visit to the Far East, Farnsworth wrote, "After such a charming approach, it is difficult for me to be so ungracious as to dodge your follow up."[520] Continuing in the same vein, he stated, "Because, I suspect, it is not for my blue eyes that you wish to see me in New York later on."[521] Therefore, Farnsworth declared, he would be "happy" to see Dr. Hume in the city, but, "again at the grave risk of seeming ungracious," he insisted that the conversation be restricted to an individual named Paul Harrison and to "your no doubt interesting trip."[522]

Equally direct was Dr. Farnsworth's response in 1938 to inquiries from Franklin W. Johnson, President of Colby College in Waterville, Maine, regarding possible support. To this college president, Farnsworth wrote, "I do not believe you are ignorant of what he [William Bingham] is doing at Gould Academy and for

Rural Medicine; these interests absorb every dollar of his that I can scrape together and will continue to so for many years."[523]

Furthermore, in his efforts to shield Will Bingham from contact with the public, Dr. Farnsworth could be quite unequivocal. For example, to a Mr. Higgins from Emerson College in Boston, who claimed to have known someone who visited Will in Bethel, he responded, "I can assure you that he never saw Mr. Bingham; I am the buffer, the filter . . . and rebuffer!"[524] He continued, "That is my job."[525] In fact, the Doctor declared, "I can assure you that if Mr. Luard got into my office, he went out again as soon as decencies would permit, with no promise of aid."[526]

Another example of Dr. Farnsworth's role as an effective "buffer" is illustrated by his response to a letter from a Miss Crayon, who wanted to send Will Bingham an account of her brother's experience with a typhoon. The Doctor assured her that this story was undoubtedly "most interesting"; however, it appeared to be "much too disturbing for a nervous invalid like Mr. B."[527] To Dr. A. S. Degg, Dean of Boston University's School of Medicine—who requested a gift of $500,000—Dr. Farnsworth replied that the request could not be approved since "no way has been found for the people of these United States to eat their cake of taxation and have philanthropy too."[528] To a correspondent from Rumford, Maine, Farnsworth observed that, in the current climate, "the philanthropist is rapidly becoming as extinct as the Dodo."[529] Another inquiry was hastily brushed aside by the Doctor, who stated that no money could be granted since Will's income had been cut in half and "it is only fair to put you out of your misery as swiftly and painlessly as possible."[530]

Every so often, Will felt compelled to express a decided opinion regarding a request. For example, an instance that "tugged" upon him concerned a plea from the Institute for the Blind in Boston for a brick dormitory for twenty men. To Dr. Farnsworth, Will wrote, "One naturally feels sympathetically inclined toward the appeal, but I agree with you that for a number of reasons, I should stand pat at present."[531] He continued by saying, "In a year or two if the need remains I should feel like looking into it seriously." Citing his present mood, however, he instructed Dr. Farnsworth to "write them that I do not feel able to take the matter up."[532]

For much of his life, Will Bingham spent most winters in Florida, a location his family had favored during his early years, since older brother Oliver—with his delicate health—found it much to his liking. The Bingham family gradually acquired and developed extensive properties there, including "Figulus," an imposing residence constructed in 1894 for Charles Bingham, and where his wife, Mary ("Molly") Payne Bingham, and son, Oliver, would pass on a few years later. As indicated earlier, Will and Oliver also owned other Florida real estate together. So it is not surprising that Will, throughout his life, felt at ease staying in Sunshine State hotels during many winters. In fact, in 1945, he acquired an Ormond Beach property (main house, orange grove, and guest cottage) to provide a comfortable place for himself and his attendants until Florida's hotels opened for the winter. Still, by the 1940s, Will was beginning to view South Florida as simply too hot. In the words of Dr. Farnsworth, Will also longed for "the remembered delights of a Bethel winter as it was in the days of the Gehrings and their interesting circle of brilliant, if emotionally unstable patients."[533] Unfortunately for Will, Farnsworth noted, "that was twenty five years ago" and "he was younger and quite physically able to battle the cold and winds and snowdrifts, and there was always a circle of unusual people to give congenial social contacts."[534] In summing up the situation, Dr. Farnsworth believed that Will "suffered greatly from loneliness and isolation last winter" and has "no taste for facing another Maine winter."[535] For that reason, the Doctor observed, Will "seems immensely cheered by his decision to go to Hotel Ormond, Ormond Beach [Florida], in my company for the four cruel months."[536] Even though George and Ruth Farnsworth were sorry to leave their coastal Maine setting to accompany Will, the Doctor noted that "when duty calls, the youth replies, I can," adding, "I'll probably live a couple extra years getting out of this d...d winter climate."[537]

One other noteworthy Florida connection was Will's interest in Rollins College at Winter Park, founded in 1885 and the Sunshine State's oldest post-secondary institution. In the early 1940s, the College was experiencing financial difficulties, and rumors reached Will that it might have to close. He was in Boston at the Ritz-Carlton at the time, and readily agreed to "protect a loan" Rollins had with a New York bank by advancing the College $10,000 "without interest or collateral."[538] This arrangement evidently kept the College going for a year or two, but a plea for funds received in 1942 was refused by Will due to increased taxation.[539]

As has been fully demonstrated, a philanthropist constantly faces all kinds of requests, proposals, and pleas for funds. Perhaps one of the more unusual appeals to William Bingham occurred in 1938 when author Charles Waterman requested a loan of $1000 to publish his proposed "History of Oxford County," which he had recently completed. Then eighty, Waterman claimed to have spent his life savings on his wife's last illness and had no money, pleading through a series of letters for Will's involvement, which was strongly opposed by Dr. Farnsworth. The author was determined to get the text before Will, but Dr. Farnsworth was equally adamant about thwarting Waterman's effort. The Doctor wrote to his friend and attorney Ellery C. Park, saying that he did not think much of the manuscript, and implored Park, when he saw Waterman, to convince him that Will could not afford $1000 for such purposes, since "relief of human suffering and education take all of Mr. Bingham's money."[540] Waterman remained persistent, however, proposing, in yet another letter, to dedicate the book to Will, at the same time scolding him for "tossing" $20,000 into the "hopper" of a political party to pay off its debt.[541] (In a marginal note on this letter, Will corrected Waterman's contention, stating that his contribution had been only $10,000.)[542] In the same letter, Waterman also posed the question to Will of the usefulness of sending students to college, when job prospects were so slim due to the Great Depression.[543] He even brought Gould Academy's Headmaster Emeritus, Frank Edward Hanscom, into the discussion by noting that the former school principal "knows something about me, should you wish to consult him."[544] (Waterman's small, 90-page book, *The Oxford Hills and Other Papers*, had been issued in a limited printing in 1929.) It is not clear whether Waterman ever got an opportunity to present his case to Will Bingham, even though Dr. Farnsworth said he would be given the opportunity if he called and made an appointment, insisting dramatically, "you shall not be condemned, unheard."[545] In the end, the book was never published, but Will wrote on one of Waterman's letters that he wished to obtain a copy for himself and one for the Bethel Inn.[546]

Will Bingham's close interest in the Bethel Inn spanned a forty-year period, from the time of its opening in 1913 to just before his death in 1955. During the time, he was its major financial benefactor and the leading figure in overseeing its operations. He took a personal interest in its fortunes, knew many of its longtime personnel, and insisted on the highest standards in its management. Yet, despite Will's keen interest in the Bethel Inn, it never really made a profit during his lifetime! Instead, its success was often measured by the size of its deficits—which Will dealt with as they came along. Naturally, questions of accounting systems, insurance issues, and personnel sometimes resulted in disagreements between Dr. Farnsworth and attorney Sidney Davidson, who became Will's primary legal adviser by the mid-1930s. From this time until Farnsworth's death in 1947, there were occasional flare-ups that disturbed the uneasy relationship between these two strong-minded individuals vying for influence with Will. Usually the turf battles involved legal issues, with Davidson standing for explicit resolution to every question and for decisions to be made in New York, while Dr. Farnsworth argued for judgements to come from the Bingham "office," wherever it might happen to be at a given time (including

Florida, Bethel, Christmas Cove, or any number of other places along the Atlantic coast).

In 1940, George Farnsworth attempted to install his attorney son-in-law, Neal Dale, as his successor, but he encountered strong resistance from Sidney Davison and his law partners. This situation was eventually resolved by Dale's resignation to enter the U.S. Navy. It's clear that Dale was held in high regard by Will, since he instructed Dr. Farnsworth to pay the difference between Dale's Navy pay and what he was receiving as part of the Bingham staff. In a letter to Will in 1942, Dr. Farnsworth said of Davidson, "I find Sid as ever legalistic."[547] He went on to observe, "He can't conceive that I would serve you for love."[548] In essence, Farnsworth was not convinced that Will's affairs, which included very detailed data gathering in connection with financial assistance, could be handled "by a junior clerk in SWD's law office."[549]

The resentment that each of these two trusted Bingham advisors held toward each other is particularly evident in an earlier letter Dr. Farnsworth wrote to Will in 1939, where he reported that he and Davidson had just had a "heavy session on fourteen points of your affairs."[550] From this encounter, Farnsworth assured Will that he was "more than ever convinced that any attempt to do this [carry on Will's affairs] through a purely legal office would end up in frustration."[551] Farnsworth went on to make the case for a manager that sounded remarkably familiar: "Only a particular type of man can handle with knowledge and intelligence" this assignment, adding, not surprisingly, a "person such as myself (with essential university teaching, medical knowledge and sociological practical outlook) would have to be the medium through which your trustees carried out your wishes."[552]

Over two years later, Dr. Farnsworth, writing from Farnstede, his "farm" in Damariscotta, Maine, was still grumbling to Will about Sidney W. Davidson's treatment of his son-in-law:

You will recall that SWD feared the creation of a dynasty directing your affairs, when we brought Neal in. He made it perfectly
clear to Neal that he would oust him at the first opportunity. He
need not have shown his hand at such length; I needed Neal at
the time of my poor and uncertain health; I doubt if, had I failed
then, you could have held Neal longer than was right and fair to
you to bring a new deal for your safety and protection. Neal was
too young, too ambitious, too much a man to limit himself at
his then age to take such a job as a way of life. He would have
stood by you loyally, for your immediate needs in a prolonged
emergency, but would also have had to develop a life of his own,
for his manhood sake. No other type of young man would have
been worth a tinker's damn to you, which is a paradox [as] when
I came to you, I had lived my active life, had proved myself, and
I was ready to enjoy a new and broader, mature experience in
philanthropy and education.[553]

By late 1943, with disagreements having become the status quo,
Sidney Davidson had fired another "salvo" at Dr. Farnsworth.
According to Farnsworth's reply to Davidson, he (Farnsworth)
proposed that all student loans over $3000 "should be forgiven,"
and all those under $3000 forgiven in 1943. Evidently, sometime in
March of 1942, the "collection of unforgiven notes disappeared"
from one of Farnsworth's several offices in use at the time. Dr.
Farnsworth's reaction to this embarrassing situation was to request
that Davidson come up with "a formula for Mr. Bingham's use."
This plea from Farnsworth led Davidson, Will's attorney, to vent
his frustrations over Farnsworth's very personal and sometimes
inconsistent guidelines for Bingham scholarship assistance. In
response to Farnsworth's letter, Davidson declared that the Doctor
was "wrong" in insinuating that his position on student loans was
"ingenuous." Davidson affirmed that he was "absolutely sincere,"
stating that he had never known "what policies controlled the making or administration of these loans or what philosophy underlay

them." In fact, Sidney Davidson believed he had been deliberately "kept in the dark" about the Bingham loan policies and procedures.

Undoubtedly, the "battle royal" between Sidney Davidson and Dr. George Farnsworth was exacerbated by the addition of Miss Dora Anthony to Will's charitable expenses (see p. 77). In a September 1940 memo from Dr. Farnsworth to Will, the Doctor noted that he was "looking forward to our daily contacts which are so much value in maintaining our complete understanding." In this instance, Dr. Farnsworth needed every bit of Will's "complete understanding," since Miss Anthony was a distant cousin of Ruth Farnsworth's mother. As mentioned earlier, her assets had been wiped out in the Great Depression of the 1930s, and her income as a piano teacher diminished by the loss of students at the onset of World War II. To alleviate this distress, Ruth Farnsworth encouraged Miss Anthony to move from New York City to Cleveland Heights where she would be nearer them. Ruth and her husband, Dr. Farnsworth, also invited Miss Anthony to spend summers with them at Christmas Cove over a period of several years, and had assisted her financially. Undoubtedly Farnsworth became anxious that if anything happened to him, his wife would not be able to maintain this support, so he turned to Will. This situation brought Sidney Davidson into the discussion, allowing him to raise uncomfortable questions about Dr. Farnsworth's operations and expenses. The whole subject of nepotism and what Davidson considered inflated travel expenditures of the staff greatly troubled him. His solution included a proposal calling for all of these charitable donations to be contracted out, with copies of the agreements sent to his office in New York. Dr. Farnsworth found it convenient not to resist this idea, though, as far as can be determined, there never were any contracts written up. Thereafter, an uneasy "truce" existed between the two men that was only resolved by Dr. Farnsworth's sudden death in 1947.[554]

In regard to management of the Bethel Inn, tensions between George Farnsworth and Sidney Davidson were often evident. Dr.

Farnsworth never appeared to be satisfied with the Inn's operations and was disturbed by its continuing deficits. In contrast, Sidney Davidson often praised the Inn's operations and, as early as 1937, pointed out to Dr. Farnsworth that the audit for the Bethel Inn revealed that much of the loss recorded was depreciation expense, which, if deducted, showed a much more modest figure in regard to business losses.

One of the post-war issues facing the Bethel Inn was its possible sale. Dr. Farnsworth viewed this prospect with some favor, providing that the proper party could be found to carry on in the same manner as Will had insisted upon since 1913. Sidney Davidson seemed very skeptical of any sale, since—in his view—divestment of the Inn might have an adverse effect on Will's other properties in Bethel, on Gould Academy, and the Town of Bethel. In fact, Davidson warned, a new owner could change the Inn to "a roadhouse with plenty of jazz, liquor, etc."[555] This change, he claimed, would be "unfavorable to Gould particularly."

Dr. Farnsworth was also suspicious of interest in the acquisition of the Bethel Inn by a former resident of Locke's Mills, a village near Bethel in the adjoining town of Greenwood. Dana Grant, who was once helped by a former Gehring patient, Horace S. Sears, in making a fortune on Wall Street, was the individual in question. Grant was in his early fifties at this time and looking for a hotel to acquire. According to Dr. Farnsworth, Grant became a friend of his mother, Mrs. Gehring, who helped him connect with Sears. Even so, a name on the letterhead of Grant's firm, "Walburger, Grant & Company," immediately raised some "red flags" for the Doctor. In a hand-written note on the bottom of this letter, Farnsworth drew attention to the name "Walburger," suggesting it designated "a Nigger in the woodpile," or, in other words, "Jewish money seeking another Maine hotel"; therefore, he advised "great caution to be observed."[556]

The likely sale of the Bethel Inn at this time resulted in much discussion among Will's key advisors—Dr. Farnsworth, Sidney

Davidson, and Joseph Barr—the latter of whom had recently joined the exclusive group of consultants due to his engineering and construction expertise. A tentative price of $375,000 was discussed and presented to Dana Grant, who did not appear to be troubled by that figure. However, in a letter to Sidney Davidson, Dr. Farnsworth reported his fear that Will would "violently oppose any change in status quo of his Bethel holdings during his lifetime" unless a strong argument could be made to the contrary.[557] Farnsworth again brought up the question of a "front" for "the flood of Jewish money buying up everything available in Maine in the hotel line."[558] He observed that Grant's letters "seem almost too naïve and simple to be true," and that it was difficult to "believe that a man who climbed from Locke Mills to a NYC partnership could possibly think of retiring at 51 and investing his capital in such a proposition as the Inn on his own."[559] He again urged caution to Davidson, since, he emphasized, "so much is at stake."[560]

In a subsequent letter to Joseph Barr, Dr. Farnsworth reported that Will Bingham appeared to have no objection to the sale of the Inn, but harbored doubts that someone with no experience in hotel management could make a success of operating it. Nevertheless, Farnsworth noted that Will smiled when informed that Dana Grant might be an agent for Jewish money.[561] The Doctor then informed Barr that Will agreed with him (Farnsworth) that he would "rather tear down the Inn than let Jewish money in."[562] He closed the letter by raising legal questions regarding the Inn's future and set forth the observation that Grant, at fifty-one, would probably outlive Will, who was then sixty-six. Ultimately, nothing ever came of all this speculation, and the Bethel Inn remained under Will's ownership at the time of his death in 1955.

One other item involving the Bethel Inn that attracted wide attention in the Bethel community and involved attorneys Sidney Davidson and Ellery Park, Bethel Inn manager Sam Blackwood, Dr. Farnsworth and Will Bingham himself was a case of arson on the Inn's property in November 1938. A small structure ("Pine Hill

Camp") was alleged to have been burned down by a man in his twenties and a woman in her forties. They were eventually found guilty of the crime, fined, and each given prison time.[563] Will Bingham's primary concern, and that of his associates, in this matter centered on who had given the young man permission to build a camp on Inn property and then to occupy the camp. The young man told authorities that G. L. Thurston, the Inn's grounds manager, was under the impression that Sam Blackwood had approved this arrangement. But Will, in a handwritten note, declared, "Blackwood did not directly give him permission," to which Farnsworth remarked that it was the alleged male arsonist who "who gave Thurston to understand that Blackwood gave permission."[564] In a letter to Sidney Davidson, Dr. Farnsworth urged the engagement of "the best detective agency" to be certain that this crime did not go "undetected and unpunished."[565] In another letter to Davidson, Farnsworth observed that Blackwood and Thurston did not "like each other," so communication was clearly a problem in determining who did in fact give permission.[566]

Throughout the years of Will's ownership of the Bethel Inn, various changes were considered and in several cases brought forth to reality. Properties were acquired, buildings razed or upgraded, and facilities expanded and enhanced. A large toboggan slide was developed in 1914; tennis courts and a golf course were offered the following year. William Upson's theater was also added at this time.[567] In 1928, a South Dining Room addition was completed. An annex came into being the following year when a nearby barn was extensively remodeled to provide additional guest rooms and a sitting parlor.[568] At Will's insistence, this newly created facility was named "The Harriette," in honor Harriette Cilley, the long-time supervisor of the Inn's waitresses and chambermaids.[569] A sprinkler system and modern laundry equipment were installed at the Inn during 1932.[570] In the summer of 1936, Will had extensive and grandiose plans drawn up by the Boston architectural firm of Coolidge and Carlson that would have greatly enlarged the Inn, but this major expansion never came to fruition.[571] On November 1, 1941, the Inn closed for the first time since it had opened in July 1913 for "extensive redecorating and additions," work that was carried out over that winter.[572]

One of the more unusual projects briefly funded by Will Bingham during World War II—undoubtedly at the insistence of Dr. Farnsworth—was the surveillance of alleged Communist infiltrators in Maine. In a letter to Will (probably from Christmas Cove, Maine), George Farnsworth stated that Republican U.S. Senator Ralph O. Brewster of Dexter, Maine, had asked him for assistance in monitoring Communist infiltration of labor unions and other "suspicious" groups in the Pine Tree State.[573] Senator Brewster, a protégé of conservative Republican Ohio Senator Robert Taft, and later an avowed follower of Senator Joseph McCarthy in his anti-communist crusade, had also served in the House of Representatives and as Governor of Maine (1925-29).[574] The Senator recommended Hugh S. Kelley of Yarmouth, Maine, to carry out the "spying" on alleged "subversives." In July 1941, Dr. Farnsworth assured Will that this activity had the approval of the Federal Bureau of Investigation, and he sought Will's approval to pay Kelley $75 per week as an "undercover investigator," with a weekly expense account of $25.[575] He assured Will that no checks bearing his signature would be issued, and that he (Farnsworth) considered this project of "enormous importance to the State, to industries and to homeowners such as you and I."[576] He then proceeded to inform Will that the "Communistic situation here in Maine is beyond belief," and declared to his superior that the situation was "thoroughly understood by me as who had been following it closely for some time."[577] He recommended this course of action "as strongly as possible."[578] Will officially assented to the arrangement the next day, on July 16, 1941.

In the fall of 1941, Hugh Kelley received authorization from Farnsworth to engage "three spotters" for a period of two weeks for about $10 per week.[579] He also received permission to extend operations beyond the State's borders "in conjunction with our mutual friend [Ralph Owen Brewster]."[580]

Nearly a year later, in June 1942, Kelley reported to Dr. Farnsworth that he had spent a week in Piscataquis County "running down leads furnished by a Deputy Sheriff," but "they all petered out as false alarms where Nazis are concerned."[581] He also noted that "any German or Italian person is under suspicion" and each case "must be investigated for fear of overlooking one really guilty party."[582]

As far as we can tell, only one of Hugh Kelley's reports to Farnsworth (May 29 to June 5, 1942) has survived in Will Bingham's papers, which may be more a result of the effort being abandoned by June 1942—not because there were no "subversives," but because of gas rationing imposed on December 1, 1941, approximately six months after the project received Will's authorization. The whole undertaking was ostensibly dubious from the beginning, but, as Hugh Kelley admitted to Farnsworth, "I cannot do justice to the job without gas."[583]

During the 1940s, another of Dr. Farnsworth's cares focused on bills being submitted by a Portland dentist, who had been engaged to come to Bethel to provide dental services for Will, since he (Will) wished to retain his privacy and not visit an office. In order to make this arrangement work, Will had his own dental chair and drill installed in his Bethel home. Dr. Farnsworth reviewed the invoices for the services of George J. Anderson, DDS, with Will, noting that, by mutual agreement, they were to be $100 per visit; even so, Farnsworth concluded that they were "excessive."[584] This judgment remained alive for some time despite Dr. Anderson's explanations for these long distance dentistry charges.[585]

Dr. George Bourne Farnsworth's tenure as Will Bingham's "chief of staff" came to an abrupt end with his sudden death on May 22, 1947, in the Miles Memorial Hospital in Damariscotta, Maine. There was no question as to whom would assume the responsibility for "looking after" Will since, in 1937, he had selected as his personal physician, a modest, soft-spoken Miami doctor, Arthur L. Walters. With Dr. Farnsworth's passing, the strong opinions, strident conservatism, racial and religious prejudice, and noxious bluster also disappeared. Dr. Farnsworth had created quite an elaborate organization, with various secretaries and assistants to maintain the correspondence needed to closely oversee Will's finances and his philanthropic endeavors. His struggles with Sidney Davidson, Joseph Barr, and others to maintain his hegemony over these rivals for influence with Will were now replaced with the collegial relationship that Dr. Walters would engender and maintain for the remainder of his patient's life.

The Gehring-Farnsworth legacy, as it related to Will Bingham, possessed quite a different meaning according to the views of Dr. Gehring's nephew, Edwin W. Gehring, M.D. (1876-1953). In a letter to his brother, Norman Gehring, M.D., dated September 5, 1949, Edwin Gehring included a check for his brother's birthday and proceeded to analyze the involvement of his uncle and aunt and that of Marian Gehring's son, George B, Farnsworth.[586] Edwin Gehring also enclosed a *Bulletin of the New England Medical Center*, a publication "financed—not by George Farnsworth—but William Bingham 2nd who got caught in the net of the 'Wizard of the Androscoggin' [a sarcastic slam at his uncle, J. G. Gehring] years ago and up to the time of Geordie's [Farnsworth's] death had not been able to extract himself." Edwin Gehring continued with his version of the Bingham-Gehring-Farnsworth relationship:

> The story surpasses those of the Arabian Nights, many—30 or more—years ago a young man with some mental quirks and, it is reported, a fortune of 86 millions wandered from Cleveland to Bethel to place himself under the beneficent care of then 'pioneer in psychiatry' Doctor John George Gehring. This was really a juicy morsel for George and Marian. They really got their teeth into that one and managed successfully to hold him over for Fauntleroy [George Bourne Farnsworth] who went to town

on Bingham's money in a big way, as you will note by reading the Bulletin. You probably know that Marian True Gehring's name stands out boldly in gold letters on the front (street side) of one big girl's dormitory, one of the group of beautiful buildings connected with Gould Academy. In the school's large Assembly Hall, facing the pupils as they sit in their seats, is an oil painting of the doctor (Gehring) head and bust. The big athletic house on the opposite side of the street from the Academy, large enough for indoor baseball practice, is known as the Farnsworth House and Gymnasium, whereas the real gym, standing next to the Academy building is called the William Bingham Gymnasium. It is a much less pretentious structure than either of the other buildings mentioned.

From this introduction, Edwin Gehring went on to expand his understanding of how George Farnsworth succeeded at Harvard University Medical School "where one sharpshooter, ever on the alert for boys, among whose acquaintances and friends millionaires might be counted, one Joseph Pratt, made himself very congenial and helpful to this young man in a big city and so <u>far from home</u>, and George fell for his flattery and obsequious attentions, hook, line and sinker." He recalled when his uncle, J. G. Gehring, fell ill, and "Pratt <u>flew</u> to Bethel to go to the aid of a colleague"—admitting that Dr. Pratt did not "exactly <u>push</u> the venerable psychiatrist <u>through</u> 'Death's Door,' but the poor man died." This allowed Dr. Pratt to get "himself into Bingham's and J.G.'s and Geordie' good graces." The result, according to Edwin Gehring, was that Dr. Pratt "came away with sufficient funds to build the Joseph H. Pratt Diagnostic Hospital in Boston and to maintain there a paid staff— <u>of which he is one</u>—in perpetuity." Edwin Gehring, a past president of the Maine Medical Association, pointed out that he had known "Pratt for years" since "he attends Annual Meeting of the Maine Medical Association" and that he found him to be, in his opinion, "a smooth operator."

"But," Edwin Gehring continued, "Joe was not finished yet with Geordie" since "his [Pratt's] name was stuck up for all time on a beautiful brick building in Boston." It seemed "he needed a Surgical Wing to his Diagnostic Clinic and he knew that George had complete control of Bingham's philanthropies."

"Two and two make four," Edwin Gehring wrote. "No sooner said than done." He noted that the next step was to call "George's attention to this crying need which, if it were erected would bear George's name for all time" Dr. Pratt "would personally see to that" according to Edwin, and "once more, Geordie took a nose-dive and behold the Farnsworth Surgical Building on [page] nine of the Bulletin."

At this point, Edwin Gehring returned to the subject of his uncle's death in 1932 and how "Geordie" had then taken over Will Bingham's affairs. He recalled how J. G. Gehring had once "in conversation" called his step-son "a fool" and that, according to attorney Ellery C. Park, Dr. Farnsworth was drawing "$75,000 yearly for directing Bingham's philanthropies."[587]

Continuing in the same vein, Edwin went on to declare that he had "no desire to detract from any ability George may have had," but did observe that Dr. Farnsworth was "four years younger than I, when I was at the Gehring house in Bethel" and "couldn't drive a nail or harness a horse or distinguish a weed from a desired plant to save his soul." Despite these deficiencies, in Edwin's view, "without any mechanical ability, he was 'called' to Cleveland to become Assistant Professor of Obstetrics at Western Reserve [University], and, when his stepfather died, he relinquished obstetrics pronto to become business manager for a multimillionaire, never having a day's business training or experience." This was a "Believe it or Not" state of affairs in the Ripley tradition, he asserted, noting that Tom Clark went to the U.S. Supreme Court "without a day's judicial experience" and J. Howard McGrath became U.S. "Attorney General without ever having a case in court."

Edwin Gehring furthered his comments to his brother by noting that "the credit for the many things Bingham's money has accomplished really belongs to the men who made it and then gave it
to Bingham." Moreover, he maintained, the money belonged "to
Bingham and then to J. G. [Gehring] for holding the man over the
years." However, he pointed out, "The names that are blazoned for
posterity to see are Pratt, Farnsworth and Marian True Gehring,"
and he predicted "most persons who read these names won't know
that Bingham ever existed."

Finally, he observed in closing that John George Gehring "was
the sickly one of grandfather's brood, who had to be sent to bed
for his rest while our father had to hold a candle for the old man to
dress his cattle into the wee hours of the morning." As a result, he
declared, John George "died in his seventies, a fakir; our father at
38, of tuberculosis, but an honest man." At the same time, he
added, "don't forget Marian" since "she had much to do, I am sure,
with making George [her husband] and Geordie [her son] stuffed
shirts and crooked, but she had good material to work with."

In a postscript, Gehring declared that his letter was "not sour
grapes" and requested that Norman send it on to their brother,
Victor. It's important to note that Edwin Gehring's credibility as an
observer of family dynamics is based, to a certain extent, on the fact
that he graduated from Gould Academy, Bowdoin College and the
Cornell University Medical School. He practiced medicine for over
half a century in Portland, Maine. A past president of the Maine
Medical Association, Cumberland County Medical Association, and
the Portland Medical Society, he also served for twenty-two years
on the Board of Overseers of the American College of Physicians,
and from 1928 to 1938 was the Chief of Medical Staff at Maine
General Hospital in Portland.[588] In other words, he had a
distinguished career and was apparently widely respected. He never
benefited directly, so far as is known, from Will Bingham's philanthropic grants and gifts. The only caveat to this statement is that
the Maine General Hospital may have received from time to time

financial support from the Bingham Associates Fund to upgrade its offerings and services, but this support would not have benefited Edwin Gehring directly.

Life with Dr. Walters

ARTHUR LOUIS WALTERS was born on January 20, 1884, in Battle Ground, Indiana, where he attended local schools and then went on to graduate at age twenty in 1904 with a B.S. from Purdue University. He received his M.D. from Johns Hopkins School of Medicine eight years later. At age thirty, in 1914, he married the former Louise Bitting (1889-1970), and that union produced two daughters and a son.[589] His wife met her future husband while she was attending the Johns Hopkins University School of Nursing in Baltimore. During World I, Dr. Walters served as a Lieutenant in the U.S. Army Medical Corps. Dr. Walters and his wife both maintained a life-long passion for gardening and horticulture, and are recalled by their grandsons as a gracious couple who enjoyed games of canasta and bridge with their neighbors while they smoked their Pall Mall's and served up drinks of lemonade, beer, and mixed beverages.

According to local historian Eva Bean, Dr. Walters arrived in Bethel as a tourist in 1934 and remained a summer resident there from 1947 to 1956. Toward the end of his life, he owned a house on Broad Street near Will's residence. Among his hobbies was the collecting of tools and tales of early Bethel. He subsequently acquired an impressive collection of eighteenth and nineteenth century antiques, some of which were stored at the Academy at the time of his death.

During the 1920s, Dr. Walters was on the pharmaceutical staff of Eli Lilly Company and became interested in the use of insulin in the treatment of diabetics. In 1924, he helped establish St. Francis Hospital in Miami Beach, Florida, where he assumed duties as its first physician-in-chief.

It is unclear how Walters came to know Will Bingham, but it is likely they met in Miami. Be that as it may, by 1932 Dr. Walters was so well-connected with Will and his inner circle that he became one of the original trustees of the Bingham Associates Fund. In 1938, with the establishment of the Pratt Diagnostic Clinic in Boston, Dr. Walters was selected as a charter trustee of the New England Medical Center.

In 1955, Will made one of the last gifts during his lifetime to Gould Academy for a student infirmary that he insisted be named for Dr. Walters. The Doctor had previously been elected to the Gould Board of Trustees in 1947 and later became Vice President of that body. Just prior to Will's death, he was added as a trustee to the Bingham Trust for Charity. In 1955, he also became a trustee of the Bingham Betterment Fund, along with Sidney Davidson and Ralph Lowell. Dr. Walters died unexpectedly at home in Miami Beach on January 25, 1961. His wife survived him by nine years, dying in 1970.

In 1937, Will Bingham became seriously ill. It was at that time that Dr. Farnsworth confronted the reality that, since his specialty was obstetrics, an internal medicine specialist should be recruited to care for Will whenever the need arose. This search did not have to go very far afield, since Dr. Walters possessed the appropriate medical training and was already part of Will's inner circle of trusted advisers.

Dr. Walter's "management style" was far less strident and pervasive than Dr. Farnsworth's "complete control regimen" that began in the early 1930s with the failing health of Dr. Gehring and continued until Farnsworth's death in May 1947. Dr. Walters usually met each day with Will in the late morning for an hour or so. It was during this time that the two men reviewed any issues and/or correspondence that needed attention and disposed of it without much fanfare. Gone was the posturing, micromanaging, and "drama" that had characterized Will's life under Dr. Farnsworth's "iron" rule. It is impossible to determine just how Will reacted to Dr. Farnsworth's passing, aside from the references to being "upset" with this loss. Dr. Walter's relationship with Will resembled the one he had experienced with Dr. Gehring, the mantra being "there if you need me," rather than the "everything has to go through me" motto of Dr. Farnsworth's era, where he so frequently emphasized his "Chief of Staff" status.

Sometimes, Dr. Walters did take the initiative to change Will's location in an attempt to improve his outlook. For example, in 1948, Walters persuaded Will to leave the Sheraton Plaza Hotel in Florida for the Hotel Ormond in the expectation that the "change in environment will produce some improvement" in his mood.[590] There appears to be no record that this relocation had the desired result, but it does demonstrate that Dr. Walters was sensitive to Will's varying moods and, like Dr. J. G. Gehring, employed a variety of strategies to ease his stresses.

When Dr. Walters took over from Dr. Farnsworth in May 1947, he generously wrote one of Will's friends that his predecessor's death "was a great shock to all of us."[591] He praised the late Doctor for his "wide outlook on everything, especially pertaining to Mr. Bingham."[592] Noting that Dr. Farnsworth had planned for this succession in regard to Will "if anything happened to him," he confided to his correspondent that he had been up to Maine "delving into the intricacies of Mr. Bingham's affairs, and taking care of a good deal of correspondence."[593] He admitted that he "was sorry to give up [his] practice and contacts in Miami Beach for this new position," but he was "sure it will open up many new fields of absorbing interests."[594] Moreover, he guessed that he would "eventually be pleased with the change."[595]

Working closely with Sidney Davidson, Joseph Barr and other trusted advisors to Will, Dr. Walters established a collegial relationship with these men and others. Scholarship lists for Gould

Academy graduates were assembled each year and approved without all the excessive belaboring that had characterized life under Dr.
Farnsworth. Betty Burns Thurston retained her unique role of
reporting on needy local cases requesting Will's support, but these
occasions appeared limited and for the most part were funded
without great "fanfare" and/or the moral preaching attached to
such cases in Dr. Farnsworth's day. And unlike Dr. Farnsworth, Dr.
Walters and Sidney Davidson worked harmoniously on all kinds of
matters relating to Will's philanthropies, including Gould Academy
and Tufts New England Medical Center. Dr. Walters lived in Bethel
during the summer and, along with his wife, was widely respected
in the town.

During his lifetime, Will Bingham—always the passionate
connoisseur—collected a significant number of works of art (many
of them western American landscapes), as well as thirty-nine
Chinese paintings that were later donated to Maine's Bowdoin
College in 1942.[596] It is known that as late as May 1954, Will was
still assisting artists in making a living. Such was the case of Frank
Wilber Stokes, about whom Will's advisors (Dr. Walters and Sidney
Davidson) conferred to determine how much to pay Stokes for one
hundred fifty paintings on canvas and one hundred thirty five on
cardboard.[597] Toward the end of his life, under Dr. Walter's
supervision and advice, Will gave a number of works from his art
collection to several academic institutions, including Princeton
University.

In addition to works of art, Will also made gifts to assist
building construction in Maine at Colby and Bowdoin colleges. In
Colby's case, a grant of $15,000 from the Bingham Trust for Charity
in 1950 assisted in the completion of a biology facility, the David
K. and Mary Arey Building for Life Sciences, which was dedicated
on October 3, 1952.[598] Sidney Davidson, a member of the Trust for
Charity Board, who had summer ties to Sebec, Maine, worked
smoothly with Colby officials in carrying out Will's predilection for
making certain all new buildings receiving his financial support were

fireproof. [599] In Colby's case, there existed another positive connection for Will, as the Life Sciences building was being constructed by Joseph Barr's New York firm.

It's interesting to note that Colby College's earlier inquiries and entreaties to Will for financial support in the Farnsworth era had not been successful. In fact, Dr. Farnsworth in one instance was forced into a "mea culpa" mode for his reaction to Colby President J. Seelye Bixler's attempt at communicating with Will Bingham. In a letter to the Colby president in 1944, the Doctor noted that he had heard from "a little bird" that he had "hurt you by my generally known and usually understood abruptness."[600] Expressing his regret, he recalled the day that Dr. Bixler had phoned, saying he wanted to see Mr. Bingham. "I seemed to have shut off that suggestion without the explanation that you, as a newcomer, should have received," Farnsworth wrote.[601] "It is generally known that Mr. Bingham does not receive any but his old friends and never anyone connected with an eleemosynary institution, as a defense against whom I hold my job," he explained.[602] Farnsworth acknowledged that he was "shocked at your perfectly innocent suggestion" and "forgot for the moment that you are newly among us."[603] He also admitted that he "recoiled in some horror at the picture of your driving up to his door and quite inevitably turned away as your status became known."[604] He wished to "save" Dr. Bixler from "a possible unnecessary diversion" since as he assured him, "You are a nice person and you are bearing such a heavy load so gallantly."[605]

Dr. Bixler was gracious in his acknowledgement of Farnsworth's letter. He noted that he understood "that you have to protect Mr. Bingham from the many demands made upon him" and also claimed to comprehend the need to curb spending in light of the increasing burden of heavy taxation.[606]

Bixler's predecessor as Colby president, Franklin Johnson, attended the dedication of Gould Academy's Farnsworth Field House in the fall of 1940. In his letter of response to President Johnson's congratulations, Dr. Farnsworth repeated his regret that the swimming pool had to be eliminated due to financial restraints, and along with it his dream that all female Gould students execute a swan dive as a condition for graduation.[607]

Earlier that fall, Dr. Farnsworth had written E. W. Millett, Assistant Director of Physical Education at Colby, his assurance that Will Bingham would have given funds to assist in building a gym ten years before, but now the outlook is "dark for philanthropies." He cited how he and Will had "rushed" to construct the Farnsworth Field House right after the boys' dormitory (Holden Hall) at Gould Academy "while we had the money and before income and capital should be taxed away."[608] He expressed strong admiration for Colby, but ended his letter with a regretful, "Sorry we cannot help."[609]

In regard to Bingham-related projects at Bowdoin College, Parker Cleveland Hall, a chemistry building designed by McKim, Mead and White, was constructed in 1951-52 by Joseph Barr's firm with funds totaling $700,000 from many sources, including a $15,000 gift from the William Bingham Trust for Charity.[610] This transaction was ably supervised by Attorney Davidson on Will's behalf and facilitated by Dr. Walters.

In his letter of thanks for the donation for Parker Cleveland Hall, Harry Palmer, '04, Executive Director of Bowdoin's Sesquicentennial Fund and a contemporary at Bowdoin of George Bourne Farnsworth, '03, made a plea for funds in support of a hockey rink in memory of Farnsworth.[611] In making this request, he cited the words inscribed at Gould Academy's Farnsworth Field House of "sound minds in sound bodies."[612] Earlier, Bowdoin president Kenneth Sills, after thanking Will Bingham for his gift for Parker Cleveland Hall, attempted to ingratiate himself with the philanthropist by noting that he had received an honorary degree from Tufts and was glad that Will was helping there, as Bowdoin had donated its medical library to that institution when it closed its medical school in 1921.[613]

While all this attention was being directed to Will from Bowdoin College, Sidney Davidson also was urging Dr. Walters to discuss with Will the suggestion of making some donation to that institution in memory of Dr. Farnsworth.[614] While he believed that Dr. Farnsworth had held "mixed" views about his alma mater, he stressed that Farnsworth possessed "a real affection for his old college and for many of his contemporaries there," as well as for President Sills.[615] Davidson also noted that Dr. Farnsworth "never pressed the needs of Bowdoin"; despite these entreaties, in the end no gift to Bowdoin in Farnsworth's memory was ever made by Will Bingham. [616]

Just as Dr. Farnsworth had to cope with Will's changing moods, so Dr. Walters was often confounded with his patient's varying mental conditions and levels of contentment. Florida itself was sometimes the answer in Dr. Farnsworth's day, but in later years, Dr. Walters insisted on moving Will from one Florida hotel to another, which often proved beneficial. This protocol did not always obtain the desired results, since, in 1953, it was not until Will reached his Bethel summer home that, in Dr. Walters' words, "he has improved and is back to his usual state of health."[617]

Two examples of Will's interaction with youngsters provide certain insights into his personality. As a neighborhood boy of six or seven years, John P. Howe III lived near Will and later recalled being on his red and white tricycle when Will strolled down Broad Street in front of the Howe residence. Will stopped and asked what John wanted to be when he grew up. Young John told him he wanted to be a doctor, and Will encouraged him to do so. He then resumed walking again after, in Howe's words, "putting a dime in my hand." It is impossible to determine if this subtle encounter influenced John's later development, but he did indeed go on to become a cardiologist.[618]

In addition, Dr. Walter's grandson, Peter McWilliams, fondly recalled his visits to Bethel in the 1950s and his grandfather's "devoted" care of "Mr. Bingham."[619] Sometimes, he wrote, his grandparents, other family members, and "Mr. Bingham" would "sit in the sun or in the shade of some pine trees in the rear of Mr. Bingham's yard, which was contiguous with a fairway of the [Bethel Inn] golf course."[620] Will Bingham appeared to this Walters grandson as "a constant summertime presence in the life of the Walters family and an occasional presence in mine during our family's continual summer trips to the idyllic town of Bethel."[621] Peter McWilliams continued:

> Often Mr. Bingham was accompanied by a female nurse. He seemed very old and quite reticent. Yet he always inquired of me and appeared to be entertained by my mumbled responses to his questions. I was too young, however, for our conversations to be termed substantial. His skin was as pale as the hide of a baseball. Never did he rise from the Adirondack chair that was provided for him in lieu of a wheelchair. Invariably, Mr. Bingham and Dr. Walters would engage in conversation of a business or medical nature that seemed irrelevant to this almost twelve-year old. But it was obvious that the medical talk revolved around Mr. Bingham's health situation and that his condition was not good.[622]

Whether or not Will Bingham was fully aware of his declining health at this time can never be known for certain, but he had sold all his Florida property by the end of 1954 and moved his banking to a Bethel institution.

When the end came for Will, he was in a Miami Hospital with his sister, Frances Bolton, by his bedside as the only family member present. Dr. Walters was also in attendance. Will died quietly and peacefully on February 17, 1955, during the evening. An autopsy was performed, revealing wide-spread cancer in the glands of the abdomen. In a letter written to Betty Burns Thurston a few days after Will's death, Dr. Walters declared that, in light of such "widespread cancer," it was "fortunate that Mr. Bingham did not linger on."[623]

Will's body was moved from Miami to Cleveland, accompanied by his sister, Elizabeth Blossom, and her son, Dudley, and his wife. It was held at the home of his nephew, Kenyon C. Bolton, until the funeral could be arranged. The funeral was held in Cleveland at Lake View Cemetery's Wade Memorial Chapel on Monday, February 21, with burial beside his parents in that cemetery.

In Bethel, following his sister Elizabeth Blossom's wishes, cash contributions to the cancer fund were encouraged in lieu of flowers. From the Bethel Inn staff and the Bingham household, a total of $26 was raised in his memory.[624] A bouquet of yellow roses and blue iris in Will's honor was placed in the Congregational Church by Betty Burns Thurston on the Sunday after his death. Later, these flowers were distributed to shut-ins by Mrs. Thurston. At the 1955 Gould Academy Alumni dinner in June, Dr. Walters stressed William Bingham's "sterling qualities," which had greatly benefited Gould and the town of Bethel.[625] The following year, in June 1956, a large group gathered after the Alumni Banquet at Alumni Field on the Gould campus to dedicate a memorial flag pole to Will from the Class of 1955. At a ceremony, which was presided over by Headmaster Elwood Ireland, the president of the Class of 1955, Curtney Mead, presented the flag pole to Sidney Davidson, the president of the Gould Board of Trustees. While the flag was being raised by members of the Class of 1955, the band played "To the Colors" and the national anthem to honor the memory of the school's greatest benefactor.[626]

In summing up Will Bingham's life and legacy, it is important to emphasize that he was never able to live the life he envisioned when a student. He had fervently wished to be a concert violinist, but his father thought otherwise. Music and art were his passions. He appreciated beauty in its many forms and nurtured a taste for numerous things cultural. As has been pointed out, Will's father, Charles Bingham, himself a cultured and refined man by any measure, was also driven by the need to succeed in business. Raising a son to become what he considered "a dilettante" was anathema to his values and violated strongly held beliefs in some version of the Protestant ethic. To Charles Bingham, it was perfectly acceptable to participate in the operations of cultural and historical institutions such as the Cleveland Museum of Art and the Western Reserve Historical Society as long as one did not shirk the responsibilities of being deeply involved in the family's business enterprises.

One can only speculate how Will's life might have been different had his mother and brother, Oliver, lived a normal lifespan. All sources indicate that he adored these two people who were such a vital part of his early years. Losing them and facing his father's disapproval of a musical career must have been almost unbearable.

Because Will was a sensitive and uncertain soul, one can readily understand his decade-plus of restless drifting prior to his arrival at Dr. Gehring's Bethel door in 1911. By this time, he had perhaps gained some perspective, since he had not totally given up his violin playing. The Gehrings readily offered acceptance and encouragement, something Will appeared to crave. They became, in a number ways, a positive parental and much needed influence upon his general equilibrium and his emotional status. Obviously, all of the psychological "scarring" he had endured during his earlier years left him focused on his health to such an extent that it tended toward hypochondria, especially as he deliberately limited his exposure to any socialization, be it family or friend. As he aged, he increasingly needed assurance that he was healthy and disease-free, yet there is at least one instance when, after a thorough examination, he almost seemed disappointed that he was found to be in good health.[627] In contrast, another unusual reaction often occurred when he did become ill and was hospitalized—as was the case several times during his life—when he confessed to feeling guilty that he might be taking the place of someone who needed medical intervention more critically than he.[628] Finally, his fear of being alone during the last twenty years of his life, and his requirement to have twenty-four hour supervision by various nurses and other medical attendants, pointed to his acute sense of isolation. Yet he remained engaged in all kinds of philanthropic endeavors throughout this time, though doctors Gehring, Farnsworth and Walters invariably had to constantly stay aware of his mental state before bringing any issues of consequence before him.[629]

Will Bingham spent much of his later life trying to be useful in some way to a multitude of people and institutions. His mind was observed by those who knew him well as keen and logical. His memory for details appeared extraordinary, and he lived rather simply for one of his means, moving up and down the east coast— usually by private rail car—from Maine (summer) to Florida (winter), with stops in between at such places as Boston, New York, Williamsburg, and the Carolinas.[630] He was known to possess a sense of humor and an ability to ask penetrating questions. In addition, for many years, Will, who was never known to have learned to drive, paid his chauffeur a generous salary, with the stipulation that the driver was to purchase and insure a car and buy a new one whenever necessary.[631] In this way, Will—always the pragmatist—would not be responsible in case of an accident, since the car would have belonged to and was insured by the chauffeur.

Will Bingham's manner has been described as "deliberate" and "unhurried" during his many discussions with his financial advisors regarding gifts of all sizes and for a multitude of purposes.[632] He approached his philanthropic endeavors with considerable thought and careful analysis. To those cases of individual need, he was most sensitive and generous, sometimes overruling advisors such as Dr. Farnsworth to expend more than recommended.

A short time after his passing, Will's sister, Frances Bolton, reflecting on his life of generosity in a letter to her sibling, Elizabeth Blossom, observed that they could not "take on Will's projects as we have many of our own."[633] The sisters appeared confident that Will had provided his "projects" with adequate funding. Frances, however, noted that "one thing he was not happy about was the

[Bethel] Inn."[634] In order to ease his mind, she had "agreed to see that it went into good hands" or her "own."[635] True to her words, Frances saw to it that the Inn was sold to a group of investors led by Guy Butler, formerly of the Maine Publicity Bureau, who maintained the highest standards during his ownership.

In an undated memo, Will Bingham once outlined the reasons why "he invested so much money in the modernization of the physical plant of Gould Academy."[636] He stated that it was not his goal "to create another first class school," since other institutions have "as much to offer" as Gould and "charge more." He understood parents "are anxious to give their children the best in education" but cannot afford the prices they would have to pay for a school comparable to Gould. "For our Bethel children," he noted, "the charge for tuition is only $100; it is fixed by law." He continued by observing that "there are plenty of fine schools already and to create one more does not interest me." "What does appeal to me," he added, "is to build up a school having a plant of the best physical equipment and having the best scholastic standards and the advantages for the building up of health, character and knowledge available at costs to those Maine children whose families have only moderate means or less, and where these children receive the best all around education." This goal, he affirmed "has been my incentive to provide such a school." He further specified that his priorities were in the following order, "first for our Bethel children, [then] for Oxford County children, and [finally] for children for all over the State of Maine." He added that he believed in "bringing in a certain amount of children from other states, with other backgrounds" as "mutually beneficial and tend[ing] to enlarge the horizons of both." But he insisted that "the school should always be primarily for Maine children," and that the document stating this wish be part of the minutes of the Gould Academy Board of Trustees.

Perhaps no one came closer to summarizing Will Bingham's lasting influence than his sister, Frances, who was the warmest family member to him, and who had once briefly joined him in seeking Dr. Gehring's care. In remarks made on October 5, 1963, during the dedication of Bingham Hall at Gould Academy, Congresswoman Bolton spoke of Will's benevolence in various parts of the world, from Istanbul, Turkey, to Santa Barbara, California:

> How far he reached out in his constant endeavor to help—how wide were his interests, how broad his sympathies [and] how deep his understanding. . . .
>
> I think this school [Gould Academy] was closest to his heart. He loved Bethel. He had an abiding respect and affection for the men and women here who were building strength and courage into warp and woof, the bricks and mortar of their young people, who in many ways had become his. He had no children of his own, but his heart encircled literally thousands.
>
> Much that he made possible will never be fully revealed, for he had no desire to be known, indeed he shrank from having his name attached to his giving. His was a stewardship seldom found and very precious. It gave him the ability to express the deep need of his soul to help people.
>
> Yes, his was a strange life, separated from the world, but it was full of quiet activities reached out into a field of dynamic action whose influence will long be felt in many places. Super sensitive, he shrank from the ugliness of the world, building a wall around himself few ever penetrated. But to him that wall was a window through which he saw with exceeding clarity the needs of men, and he did what he could to build opportunity. Yes, he was considered eccentric, but he was respected by all who shared his work. His brilliant mind, his quick grasp of the most complex matters, his amazing memory, his wise judgment—in those areas he stood head and shoulders above most men, and what wit and humor was his.[637]

In the final analysis, what "monument" would embody Will Bingham's legacy? There are "brick and mortar" examples such as the Gould Academy campus in Maine, the dormitory at Yale, and the Farnsworth medical building at Tufts New England Medical Center in Boston. There were also all the smiles that must have appeared on countless faces for generous assistance with living and medical expenses or funds to attend college, law, or medical school. Then there are all those dedicated individuals who worked closely with Will to upgrade hospitals and improve medical services in so many places. Their labors continue through the Bingham Program (successor to the Bingham Associates Fund established in 1932). Currently based in Augusta, Maine, it is administered by Tufts Medical Center and dedicated to promoting health and advancing medicine in the Pine Tree State. Finally, the three foundations that bear his name (Bingham Trust, William Bingham Foundation, and Bingham Betterment) continue to serve in various ways to advance the myriad causes he championed during his lifetime. Despite what many would consider a decidedly sad and lonely life, William Bingham 2nd's legacy, at least in part, must stand as an inspiration to those who dedicate their lives to philanthropy, doing the good work that he devoted so much of his life and energies to for so very long.

NOTES

Chapter 1: Antecedents and Early Days

1. Much of the family genealogy is based upon Ruth Lawrence, *Payne, Bingham, Bolton and Allied Family Histories: Genealogical and Biographical* (New York: National Americana Publications, 1954). Also useful for family information is William Ganson Rose, *Cleveland: The Making of a City* (Cleveland, Ohio: World Publishing, 1950), David Van Tassel and John J. Grabowski, editors, *The Encyclopedia of Cleveland History* (Bloomington: Indiana University Press, 1987), Jan Cigliano, *Showplace of America: Cleveland's Euclid Avenue, 1850-1910* (Kent, Ohio: Kent State University Press, 1991), and David Loth, *A Long Way Forward: The Biography of Congresswoman Frances P. Bolton* (New York: Longmans, Green, 1957).

2. For a brief history of Cleveland, see Carol Poh Miller and Robert Wheeler, *Cleveland: A Concise History, 1796-1990* (Bloomington: Indiana University Press, 1990).

3. Quoted in Ruth Lawrence, *Payne, Bingham, Bolton and Allied Family Histories: Genealogical and Biographical*, p. 106

4. See Cigliano, *Showplace of America*, 1-12. For the address numbers of the Charles Bingham residence, see 348 Appendix A.

5. For the history of the School, see Richard A. Hawley, *Hail University!: A Century of University School Life* (Huntington Valley, Ohio: University School, 1990).

6. Transcript, University School, 1890-1896.

7. Letter, William Bingham II to Henry B. Payne, April 2, 1890, Payne Family Archives, Cleveland, Ohio, Folder: "Letters of William Bingham II to family members, 1890-1903 & undated."

8. Letter, William Bingham II to Frances Bingham, n.d., Payne Family Archives, Cleveland, Ohio, William Bingham II Papers,

Folder: "Letters to William Bingham II to family members, 1890-1903 & undated."

9. See note 7 above.

10. Letter, William Bingham II to Oliver Bingham, April 19, 1896, Payne Family Archives, Cleveland, Ohio, William Bingham II Papers, Folder: "Letters of William Bingham II to family members 1890-1903 and undated"

11. Ibid.

12. Ibid.

13. Ibid

14. Ibid.

15. Ibid.

16. Ibid.

17. See Loth, *Long Way Forward,* p. 25

18. Email letter to author from Kathleen Brewster, Santa Barbara, California, February 6, 2011. An obituary published in the *Santa Barbara News Press*, February 24, 1955, recorded that Will Bingham spent four winters there in the 1920s and purchased a small house there.

19. Ibid.

20. Ibid.

21. Letter, William Bingham II to Henry B. Payne, December 27, 1891, Payne Family Archives, Cleveland, Ohio, William Bingham II Papers, Folder: "Letters to William Bingham II to family members 1890 and undated."

22. Letter, William Bingham II to Charles Bingham, n.d. Payne Family Archives, Cleveland, Ohio, Folder: "Letters of William Bingham II to family members, 1890-1903 and undated."

23. Letter, William Bingham II to Charles Bingham, February 28, 1892, Payne Family Archives, Cleveland, Ohio, Folder: "Letters of William Bingham II to family members, 1890-1903 and undated."

24. Ibid.

25. Ibid.

26. Santa Barbara Collegiate School Report, February 26, 1892, Payne Family Archives, Cleveland, Ohio, Folder: "Letters of William Bingham II to family members, 1890-1903 and undated."

27. Ibid.

28. Santa Barbara Collegiate School Report, January 29, 1892, Payne Family Archives, Cleveland, Ohio, Folder: "Letters of William Bingham II to family members, 1890-1903 and undated."

29. Ibid.

30. See note 21 above.

31. Ibid.

32. Ibid.

33. Ibid.

34. Ibid.

35. Ibid.

36. Ibid.

37. Ibid.

38. Letter, William Bingham II to Charles Bingham, January 23, 1892, Payne Family Archives, Cleveland, Ohio, Folder: "Letters of William Bingham II to family members, 1890-1903 and undated."

39. Ibid.

40. Ibid.

41. Ibid.

42. Ibid.

43. Ibid.

44. *The Morning Press*, Santa Barbara, March 10, 1892.

45. Letter, William Bingham II to Charles Bingham, March 18, 1892, Payne Family Archives, Cleveland, Ohio, Folder: "Letters of William Bingham II to family members, 1890-1903 and undated."

46. Letter, William Bingham II to Oliver Bingham, n.d., Payne Family Archives, Cleveland, Ohio, Folder: "Letters to William Bingham II to family members, 1890-1903 and undated."

47. Ibid.

48. Letter, William Bingham II to Oliver P. Bingham, December 18, 1895, Payne Family Archives, Cleveland, Ohio, Folder:

"Letters of William Bingham II to family members 1890-1903 and undated."

49. Ibid.

50. Ibid.

51. Ibid.

52. For details of the founding of St. Paul's, see Arthur Stanwood Pier, *St. Paul's School 1855-1934* (New York: Charles Scribner's Sons, 1934), pp. 1-15, and August Heckscher, *St. Paul's: The Life of a New England School* (New York: Charles Scribner's Son, 1980), pp. 1-19. See also "St. Paul's School, Concord, N.H." by Rev. Edward M. Parker in George Gary Bush, Ph.D., *History of Education in New Hampshire* (Washington, D.C.: Government Printing Office, 1898), pp. 93-99.

53. Letter, William Bingham II to Mary Payne Bingham, September 27, 1896, Payne Family Archives, Cleveland, Ohio, Folder: "Letters of William Bingham II 1890-1903 and undated."

54. Ibid.

55. Ibid.

56. Ibid.

57. Ibid.

58. Ibid.

59. Letter, William Bingham II to Mary Payne Bingham, October 8, 1896, Payne Family Archives, Cleveland, Ohio, Folder: "Letters of William Bingham II 1890-1903 and undated."

60. Ibid.

61. Ibid.

62. Ibid.

63. Ibid.

64. Ibid.

65. Ibid.

66. Ibid.

67. Letter, William Bingham II to Oliver Bingham, October 9, 1896, Payne Family Archives, Cleveland, Ohio, Folder: "Letters of William Bingham II to family members 1890-1903 and undated."

68. Ibid.

69. Ibid.

70. Letter, William Bingham II to Mary Bingham, October 3, 1896, Payne Family Archives, Cleveland, Ohio, Folder: "Letters of William Bingham II to family members 1890-1903 and undated."

71. See note 67 above.

72. Letter, William Bingham II to Charles Bingham, October 11, 1896, Payne Family Archives, Cleveland, Ohio, Folder: "Letters of William Bingham II to family members 1890-1903 and undated."

73. Ibid.

74. Ibid.

75. Ibid.

76. Ibid.

77. Letter, William Bingham II to Mary Bingham, October 25, 1896, Payne Family Archives, Cleveland, Ohio, Folder: "Letters of William Bingham II to family members 1890-1903 and undated."

78. Ibid.

79. Ibid.

80. Ibid.

81. See report in Payne Family Archives, Cleveland, Ohio, Folder: "Letters of William Bingham II to family members 1890-1903 and undated."

82. Ibid.

83. Ibid.

84. Ibid.

85. Letter, William Bingham II to Oliver P. Bingham, November 1, 1896, Payne Family Archives, Cleveland, Ohio, Folder: "Letters of William Bingham II to family members 1890-1903 and undated."

86. Ibid.

87. Ibid.

88. Ibid.

89. Ibid.

90. Ibid.

91. Ibid.

92. Letter, William Bingham II to Charles Bingham, November 6, 1896, Payne Family Archives, Cleveland, Ohio, Folder: "Letters of William Bingham II to family members 1890-1903 and undated."

93. Ibid, note 85.

94. Ibid.

95. Ibid.

96. Ibid.

97. Ibid.

98. Ibid.

99. Letter, William Bingham II to Mary Bingham, November 8, 1896, Payne Family Archives, Cleveland, Ohio, Folder: "Letters of William Bingham II to family members 1890-1903 and undated."

100. Ibid.

101. Ibid.

102. Ibid.

103. Ibid.

104. Letter, William Bingham II to Mary Bingham, November 15, 1896, Payne Family Archives, Cleveland, Ohio, Folder: "Letters of William Bingham II to family members 1890-1903 and undated."

105. Ibid.

106. Ibid.

107. Letter, William Bingham II to Charles Bingham, November 22, 1896, Payne Family Archives, Cleveland, Ohio, Folder: "Letters of William Bingham II to family members 1890-1903 and undated."

108. Ibid.

109. Ibid.

110. Ibid.

111. Ibid.

112. Letter, William Bingham II to Mary Bingham, November 22, 1896, Payne Family Archives, Cleveland, Ohio, Folder: "Letters of William Bingham II to family member 1890-1903 and undated."

113. Ibid.

114. Letter, William Bingham II to Oliver P. Bingham, November 27, 1896, Payne Family Archives, Cleveland, Ohio, Folder: "Letters of William Bingham II to family members 1890-1903 and undated."

115. Ibid.

116. Ibid.

117. Ibid.

118. Ibid.

119. Letter, William Bingham II to Mary Bingham, November 27, 1896, Payne Family Archives, Cleveland, Ohio, Folder: "Letters of William Bingham II to family members 1890-1903 and undated."

120. Ibid.

121. Ibid.

122. Ibid.

123. Letter, William Bingham II to Mary Bingham, undated, Payne Family Archives, Cleveland, Ohio, Folder: "Letters of William Bingham II to family members 1890-1903 and undated."

124. Ibid.

125. Ibid.

126. Ibid.

127. Ibid.

128. Ibid.

129. Ibid.

130. Ibid.

131. Ibid.

132. Ibid.

133. Ibid.

134. Ibid.

135. Letter, William Bingham II to Oliver P. Bingham, December 6, 1896, Payne Family Archives, Cleveland, Ohio, Folder: "Letters of William Bingham II to family members 1890-1903 and undated."

136. Ibid.

137. Ibid.

138. Letter, William Bingham II to Oliver P. Bingham, December 20, 1896, Payne Family Archives, Cleveland, Ohio, Folder: "Letters of William Bingham II to family members 1890-1903 and undated."

139. Ibid.

140. Ibid.

141. Ibid.

142. Ibid.

143. Letter, William Bingham II to Oliver P. Bingham, December 31, 1896, Payne Family Archives, Cleveland, Ohio, Folder: "Letters of William Bingham II to family members 1890-1903 and undated."

144. Ibid.

145. Letter, William Bingham II to Charles Bingham, January 3, 1897, Payne Family Archives, Cleveland, Ohio, Folder: "Letters of William Bingham II to family members 1890-1903 and undated."

146. Ibid.

147. Letter, William Bingham II to Mary Bingham, January 10, 1897, Payne Family Archives, Cleveland, Ohio, Folder: "Letters of William Bingham II to family members 1890-1903 and undated."

148. Ibid.

149. Ibid.

150. Ibid.

151. Letter, William Bingham II to Charles Bingham, March 21, 1897, Payne Family Archives, Cleveland, Ohio, Folder: "Letters of William Bingham II to family members 1890-1903 and undated."

152. Ibid.

153. Ibid.

154. Ibid.

155. Letter, William Bingham II to Charles Bingham, June 1, 1897, Payne Family Archives, Cleveland, Ohio, Folder: "Letters of William Bingham II to family members 1890-1903 and undated."

156. Ibid.

157. For details see Dumas Malone, editor, *Dictionary of American Biography*, XVII New York: Charles Scribner's Sons, 1932) pp. 30-31.

158. Ibid.

159. Ibid. Note 155.

160. Ibid.

161. Ibid.

162. Ibid.

163. Ibid.

164. Ibid.

165. Ibid.

166. Ibid.

167. Ibid.

168. Ibid.

169. Ibid.

170. Ibid.

171. Ibid.

172. Ibid.

173. Ibid.

174. Letter, Agnes Judson to William Bingham II, October 18, 1898, William Bingham II Papers, Payne Family Archives, Cleveland, Ohio, Folder: "Letters, July-October 1898."

175. Ibid.

176. Letter, Charles Bingham to William Bingham 2nd, September 28, 1898, William Bingham II Papers, Payne Family Archives, Cleveland, Ohio, Folder: "Letters, July-October 1898." This letter contains the reference to malaria, which may provide the basis for believing Will Bingham contracted this disease, but the evidence is scanty. Typhoid fever is also referenced in this era, but no definitive source is available.

177. Ibid.

178. Ibid.

179. Ibid.

Chapter 2: Years in the Wilderness
and Discovery of Bethel

180. Bingham, William II. Letter to George B. Farnsworth 29 July 1935. Manuscript Collection 4691, William Bingham II Papers. Western Reserve Historical Society, Cleveland, Ohio. Once he had found Fader's address, he sent him $500.

181. For historical descriptions of life in logging camps in the northern New England and the Canadian Maritimes, see Robert E. Pike, *Tall Trees, Tough Men* (New York: W. W. Norton, 1967), pp. 90-101, and David C. Smith, *A History of Lumbering in Maine 1861-1960* (Orono: University of Maine Press, 1972), pp. 16-27.

182. For some insights into Bingham's early life see Eva M. Bean Papers, Collections of the Bethel Historical Society, Bethel, Maine, "History of Gould Academy" manuscript, "Trustees" section, pp. 8-11. Also useful is Francis Parkman, *The Gould Academy Story 1836-1976* (Bethel, Maine: Gould Academy, 1976), pp. 93-95. Robert T. Barr's sketch of Will Bingham in his *William Bingham 2nd Trust for Charity/The Bingham Trust* (1992 revised ed.; privately printed; author's collection) contains a number of references to Bingham's early years and personality. Robert Barr was the son of Joseph Barr, who was part of Will Bingham's "inner circle" of advisors and trusted confidants by the 1930s.

183. For historical perspectives on bachelors in American history, see Howard P. Chudacoff, *The Age of the Bachelor: Creating an American Subculture* (Princeton, New Jersey: Princeton University Press, 1999). Also useful insights are found in E. Anthony Rotundo, "Romantic Friendship: Male Intimacy and Middle-Class Youth in the Northern United States, 1800-1900," *Journal of Social History*, 23 (Fall 1989), pp. 1-25.

184. Speech of Frances P. Bolton, Member of Congress, 22nd District of Ohio, at Dedication Ceremonies of Bingham Hall at Gould Academy, Bethel, Maine, October 5, 1963. Bethel Historical Society, Gould Academy Archives, Collection 1, Box 10.

185. Ibid.

186. Barr, *William Bingham 2nd Trust for Charity/The Bingham Trust*, p. 3.

187. Eva Bean's sketch of Bingham in her Gould Academy history manuscript cited previously makes reference to the bout with typhoid fever (page 8) and so does Francis Parkman in his Gould history (page 93), but none of the surviving letters from this period reviewed by the author contain any reference to this illness. Note 173 contains his father's reference to Will having malaria.

188. See letter, Frances P. Bolton to Eva M. Bean, February 17, 1961, Collections of the Bethel Historical Society, Bethel, Maine, Eva Bean Papers, Box 11, Folder: "Letters." This letter also records that Will "came down with typhoid fever" while at St. Paul's School.

189. The impact upon Will of his mother's death, as well as the burden of attempting to provide some consolation to a grieving father in the loss of Oliver, whom Will adored, was almost more than he could endure. Will's longing for a career as a violinist was dashed by paternal decree, which proved detrimental to his mental health. See this discussion in David Loth, *A long Way Forward: The Biography of Congresswoman Frances P. Bolton* (New York: Longmans, Green and Co., 1957) pp. 59-60.

190. Ibid.

191. Barr, *William Bingham 2nd Trust for Charity/The Bingham Trust*, p. 3.

192. Ibid, note 185. In the same letter, his sister Frances wrote of his western travels: "I think he felt himself much nearer the deeper values of the Universe when he was out in the open, among the mountains, or by the sea."

193. For details on Gehring's background, see William D. Andrews, "Dr. John George Gehring and his Bethel Clinic: Pragmatism Therapy and Therapeutic Tourism," *Maine History*, Volume 43, Number 3 (January 2008), pp. 188-216.

194. For details on Dr. True's career and influence, see Parkman, *The Gould Academy Story*, pp. 34-48.

195. See Andrews article cited in note 193, p.191.

196. Mrs. Gehring was born Susan Maria True, but later became "Marian True Gehring." Her half-sister, Mary True, the famed teacher of the deaf, always referred to her as "Susie" while Dr. Gehring called her "Mariian," but not with the usual pronunciation. It was more like "MARYan." See notes of Margaret Herrick Oakes in the Collections of the Bethel Historical Society, Bethel, Maine, Box 32, Folder: "Broad Street."

197. See Andrews article cited in note 193, p.191.

198. Ibid.

199. For details, see *The Bethel News*, February 26, 1896.

200. See Randall H. Bennett, *Oxford County, Maine: A Guide to Its Historic Architecture* (Bethel, Maine: Oxford County Historic Resource Survey, 1984), p. 44 for further details on the building.

201. See Andrews article, p. 191 and for details consult Samuel Williston, *Life and Law: An Autobiography* (Boston: Little Brown, 1941).

202. See Max Eastman, *Enjoyment of Living* (New York: Harper & Brother, 1948), pp. 258-260. For additional insights into Eastman's interaction with Gehring, see William L. O'Neill, *The Last Romantic: A Life of Max Eastman* (New York: Oxford University Press, 1978) pp. 13-14, 18, 251-252. Eastman described his treatment by Gehring in "The New Art of Healing," *Atlantic Monthly* (May 1908), pp. 664-650.

203. Many of Gehring's ideas and treatments are discussed in his *The Hope of the Variant* (New York: Charles Scribner's Sons, 1923). Also useful in understanding Gehring's dealings with his patients is T. Mitchell Prudden, "Dr. Gehring's Work at Bethel, Maine," a paper read before the Practitioners Society of New York, pp. 1-21 and Charles Driscoll, "The Miracle Man of Bethel" in *The New McClure's Magazine*, January 1929, pp. 32-33, 74, 76,78. Gehring was also reportedly greatly influenced by the work of the French psychiatrist Dr. Hippolyte Bernheim, a pioneer in the psychotherapy of the emotionally disturbed, whom he and his wife

met on one of their European trips. See also Joseph E. Garland, *An Experiment in Medicine: The First Twenty Years of the Pratt Clinic and the New England Center Hospital of Boston* (Cambridge, Massachusetts: Riverside Press, 1960), p. 2.

204. Collections of the Bethel Historical Society, Bethel, Maine, Box 11, Gould Academy manuscript. Despite this description of being outside of usual medical practices, Dr. Farnsworth characterized his step-father as "an exceedingly regular, orthodox physician" in response to one inquiry. See Farnsworth, George B. Letter to Hazel S. Anderson 2 September 1937. Manuscript Collection 4691, William Bingham II Papers. Western Reserve Historical Society, Cleveland, Ohio.

205. For additional information on Hale's experience at the Gehring clinic see, Andrews, pp. 199-205. Franklin Lane's biographical details can be found in Dumas Malone, editor, *Dictionary of American Biography*, X (New York: Charles Scribner's Sons, 1937), pp. 573-574 and Anne Wintermute Lane and Louise Herrick Wall, editors, *The Letters of Franklin K. Lane: Personal and Political* (Boston: Houghton Mifflin, 1922). Details of Charles Culberson's career are found in *Biographical Directory of the American Congress 1774-1961* (Washington, DC: Government Printing Office, 1961), p. 761.

206. Lane and Wall, eds., *The Letters of Franklin K. Lane*, p. 357-358.

207. Lane and Wall, eds., *The Letters of Franklin K. Lane*, p. 358.

208. See "The Bethel League," Collections of the Bethel Historical Society, Box 52.

209. See Note 190. See also *The Oxford County Citizen*, February 5, 1915.

210. Ibid.

211. Ibid.

212. Ibid.

213. Ibid.

214. Ibid.

215. Ibid.

216. Ibid.

217. *The Oxford County Citizen*, September 23, 1915.

218. Ibid.

219. Ibid.

220. Ibid.

221. Ibid.

222. William Fuller, who married a former patient, built a structure in the woods in back of the Gehring's home, often referred to as "Fuller's Hut." He once lived at the Bethel Inn and later resided in the house that William Bingham II would eventually acquire from Dr. Gehring in 1923. Fuller had an English valet who was killed in World War I. See Margaret Herrick Oakes, "Memories of Broad Street," Collections of the Bethel Historical Society, Bethel, Maine, Box 32, Folder: "Broad Street."

223. *The Oxford County Citizen*, September 21, 1916.

224. Ibid.

225. Ibid.

226. Ibid.

227. Ibid.

228. Ibid.

229. Gardiner Hubbard (1822-1897) met Mary True at a Bethel hotel where she was working as a waitress and asked her to come to Boston to teach Mabel. For further information on Mary True, see Eva Bean Papers, Bethel Historical Society Archives, Box 11, Gould Academy Trustees, pp. 58-59. She also became a Gould Academy trustee in 1917,

230. For details see Robert V. Bruce, *Bell: Alexander Graham Bell and the Conquest of Solitude* (Boston: Little, Brown & Company, 1973), pp. 86-87, 100.

231. See Margaret Herrick Oakes, "Memories of Broad Street," p. 8. For information on the True family, see William B. Lapham, *History of Bethel, Formerly Sudbury Canada, Oxford County, Maine 1768-1890* (Augusta, Maine: Press of the Maine Farmer, 1891), pp. 624-625.

232. Letter, Frances Bolton to William Bingham II, October 18, 1914, Payne Family Archives, Cleveland, Ohio, William Bingham II Correspondence, Folder: "1898, 1911-May 1918."

233. *The Oxford County Citizen*, July 27, 1911.

234. The Festival, held annually, was made up of choruses from throughout Maine, plus outstanding singers and orchestras of national and often international renown. Chapman, who was born in Massachusetts and spent his early years in Bethel and attended Gould Academy briefly, was descended from Rev. Eliphaz Chapman, who played a leading role in naming the town in 1796. For details on Chapman, see Mina Holway Caswell, *Ministry of Music: The Life of William Rogers Chapman* (Portland, Maine: The Southworth-Anthoensen Press, 1938).

235. See Caswell, *Ministry of Music*, p. 306.

236. *The Oxford County Citizen*, August 10, 1911.

237. *The Oxford County Citizen*, August 24, 1911.

238. *The Oxford County Citizen*, November 21, 1912.

239. *The Oxford County Citizen*, May 8, 1913

240. *The Oxford County Citizen*, July 10, 1913.

241. *The Oxford County Citizen*, March 29, 1917.

242. *The Oxford County Citizen*, June 17, 1915.

243. *The Oxford County Citizen*, November 25, 1915

244. *The Oxford County Citizen*, February 2, 1936

245. *The Oxford County Citizen*, March 21, 1912. See also Parkman, *The Gould Academy Story*, p. 95

246. *The Oxford County Citizen*, October 10, 1912.

247. *The Oxford County Citizen*, December 26, 1912.

248. *The Oxford County Citizen*, September 27, 1913. See also Parkman, *The Gould Academy Story*, p. 95. For further information on Holden, see Dumas Malone, editor, *Dictionary of American Biography* (New York: Charles Scribner's Sons, 1932), pp. 137-138.

249. *The Oxford County Citizen*, December 2, 1915.

250. The Academy's principal Frank E. Hanscom in a letter in December 1917 urged him to stay on the Board of Trustees insisting that "the prestige of your name" would be "of value to the school." Hanscom expressed gratitude to Bingham for his rescue of the Academy and what a "load it takes from me" with his offer of support since he wrote that he had "given twenty-one of his best years to Gould's Academy because he believed in the work the school is doing and has done." Letter, Frank E. Hanscom to William Bingham II, December 14, 1917, Payne Family Archives, Cleveland, Ohio, Folder: "1898, 1911 to May 1918."

251. For a discussion of the financial challenges of this era see Parkman, *The Gould Academy Story,* pp. 102-105.

252. Hanscom, Frank E. Letter to William Bingham II 22 December 1912. Manuscript Collection 4691, William Bingham II Papers. Western Reserve Historical Society, Cleveland, Ohio.

253. *The Oxford County Citizen,* April 26, 1917.

254. In a letter to his father, dated August 9, 1918, Will assured him that "Dr. Wight of Bethel is the examining medical officer for Oxford County" and "is familiar with Dr. Gehring and his work and that I have been a patient of Dr. Gehring." William Bingham II to Charles Bingham, August 9, 1918, Payne Family Archives, Cleveland, Ohio, William Bingham II Papers, Folder: "Correspondence 1918-1919."

255. For insights into the Bethel domestic scene and World War I see, Stanley Russell Howe, "War to End All Wars: Bethel During the First World War," *The Bethel Courier,* Volume II, Number 1 (December 1977), pp.1-3

256. See Howe, "War to End All Wars: Bethel During the First World War," p. 2

257. Letter, William Bingham II to the Board of Bethel Selectmen, August 16, 1918, Payne Family Archives, Cleveland, Ohio, William Bingham II Papers, Folder: "Correspondence 1918-1919."

258. Letter, William Bingham II to Charles Bingham, August 9, 1918, Payne Family Archives, Cleveland, Ohio, William Bingham II Papers, Folder: "Correspondence 1918-1919."

259. Letter, Charles Bingham to William Bingham II, August 12, 1918, Payne Family Archives, Cleveland, Ohio, William Bingham II Papers, Folder: "Correspondence 1918-1919."

260. Ibid.

261. Ibid.

262. Letter, J. G. Gehring to William Bingham II, October 21, 1912, Payne Family Archives, Cleveland, Ohio, William Bingham II Correspondence, Folder: "1898, 1911-May 1918."

263. Ibid.

264. Ibid.

265. Ibid.

266. Ibid.

267. Letter, J. G. Gehring to William Bingham II, November 1, 1912, Payne Family Archives, Cleveland, Ohio, William Bingham II Correspondence, Folder: "1898, 1911-May 1918."

268. Ibid.

269. Ibid.

270. Ibid.

271. See Letter, Charles Bingham to William Bingham II, April 18, 1918, Payne Family Archives, Cleveland, Ohio, William Bingham II Correspondence, Folder: "1898, 1911 to May 1918" and Letter, Charles Bingham to William Bingham II, May 8, 1918, Folder: "1898, 1911 to May 1918."

272. See Letter, Charles Bingham to William Bingham II, May 2, 1918, Payne Family Archives, Cleveland, Ohio, William Bingham II Correspondence, Folder: "1898, 1911 to May 1918."

273. See Letter, Frances Bolton to William Bingham II, November 10, 1917, Payne Family Archives, Cleveland, Ohio, William Bingham II Correspondence, Folder: "1898, 1911 to May 1918."

274. Ibid.

275. See Letter, William Bingham II to Charles Bingham, August 12, 1918, Payne Family Archives, Cleveland, Ohio, William Bingham II Correspondence, Folder: "1918-1919."

276. See Letter, Harry Bingham to William Bingham II, July 31, 1917, Payne Family Archives, Cleveland, Ohio, William Bingham II Correspondence, Folder: "1898, 1911 to May 1918."

277. Invoice, Grand Trunk Railway System, January 19, 1919, Payne Family Archives, Cleveland, Ohio, William Bingham II Correspondence, Folder: "1918-19."

278. See Letter, William Bingham II to Charles Bingham, April 19, 1918, Payne Family Archives, Cleveland, Ohio, William Bingham II Correspondence, Folder: "1918-19." Charles Bingham's response to Will's inquiry about the envelope is found in his letter of June 28, 1918 to Will, Payne Family Archives, Cleveland, Ohio, William Bingham II Correspondence, Folder: "1918-19."

279. Letter, George B. Farnsworth to William Bingham II, September 23, 1917, Payne Family Archives, Cleveland, Ohio, William Bingham II Correspondence, Folder: "1898, 1911-May 1918." Will Bingham also contributed $1500 to the United Committee on War Temperance. See Bingham, William II. Letter to V. L. Phillips 20 March 1919. Manuscript Collection 4691, William Bingham II Papers. Western Reserve Historical Society, Cleveland, Ohio.

280. Robert College was founded in 1863 in Turkey by two Americans: Cheslyn Robert (1802-1878), a philanthropist, and Cyrus Hamlin (1811-1900), a missionary born at Waterford, Maine. See *Dictionary of American Biography*, Dumas Malone, editor (New York: Charles Scribner's Sons, 1932), Volume VIII, pp. 195-196, and *Dictionary of American Biography*, Dumas Malone, editor (New York: Charles Scribner's Sons, 1935), pp. 81-82. For details of the college's history, see May N. Fincanci, *The Story of Robert College: Old and New*, Revised Edition (Istanbul, Turkey: InterMedia, 2001). Of particular interest regarding the gift in memory of Mary Payne

Bingham, see pages 120-127. The $500,000 gift is not mentioned in the Robert College history, but was duly noted by President Clifton D. Gray of Bates College and strengthened his resolve to persist in requesting funds for that Lewiston, Maine, institution. See note 304.

281. Memorandum, Addison E. Herrick to William Bingham II, November 20, 1918, Payne Family Archives, Cleveland, Ohio, William Bingham II Correspondence, Folder: "1918-19."

282. Letter, Walter L. Gray, Attorney at Law, South Paris, Maine to Lester H. Penley, November 10, 1924 lists the price paid as $50,000. Courtesy of Richard Penley, Paris, Maine.

283. Deed, Penley Brothers to William Bingham II, October 22, 1914, Oxford County Registry of Deeds, Paris, Maine, Box 270, p. 281.

284. Deed, William Bingham II to Bethel Water Company, March 27, 1925, Oxford Country Registry of Deeds, Paris, Maine, Book 366, pp. 453-454.

285. Ibid.

286. Ibid.

287. Ibid.

288. Ibid.

289. See Margaret Herrick Oakes, "Memories of Broad Street," *The Bethel Courier*, Vol. I, Number 2 (June 1977), p. 2. Here Mrs. Oakes notes the newspaper article that sent Will into seclusion and her memories of dancing with Will, who she recalled liked the "hesitation waltz," was known to attend "all the dances" and played the violin "beautifully."

290. Letter, "Mrs. R.C." to William Bingham II, February 4, 1916, Payne Family Archives, Cleveland, Ohio, William Bingham II Correspondence, Folder: "1898, 1911-May 1918."

291. Letter, Edward Perkins Carter to William Bingham II, October 6, 1918, Payne Family Archives, Cleveland, Ohio, William Bingham II Correspondence, Folder: "1918-19."

292. Ibid.

293. Ibid.

294. Ibid.

295. Ibid.

296. Letter, Edward Perkins Carter to William Bingham II, October 20, 1918, Payne Family Archives, Cleveland, Ohio, William Bingham II Correspondence, Folder: "1918-19."

297. Letter, William Bingham II to George Chase, April 22, 1919, Assistant to the President, Series II: Wills & Gifts, Box 1, William Bingham Correspondence, Edmund S. Muskie Archives & Special Collections Library, Bates College, Lewiston, Maine.

298. Letter, Frank E. Hanscom to Dr. Clifton D. Gray, November 22, 1922, Assistant to the President, Series II, Willa & Gifts, Box 1, William Bingham Correspondence, Edmund S. Muskie Archives & Special Collections Library, Bates College, Lewiston, Maine.

299. Ibid.

300. Ibid.

301. Ibid.

302. Letter, Dr. Clifton D. Gray to William Bingham II, December 1, 1922, Assistant to the President, Series II, Wills & Gifts, Box 1, William Bingham Correspondence, Edmund S. Muskie Archives & Special Collections Library, Bates College, Lewiston, Maine.

303. Letter, Frank E. Hanscom to Dr. Clifton D. Gray, December 14, 1922, Assistant to the President, Series II, Wills & Gifts, Box 1, William Bingham Correspondence, Edmund S. Muskie Archives & Special Collections, Bates College, Lewiston, Maine.

304. Ibid.

305. Letter, William Bingham II to Dr. Clifton D. Gray, December 11, 1922, , Assistant to the President, Series II, Wills & Gifts, Box 1, William Bingham Correspondence, Edmund S. Muskie Archives & Special Collections, Bates College, Lewiston, Maine.

306. Letter, Dr. Clifton D. Gray to William Bingham II, November 21, 1922, Assistant to the President, Series II, Wills & Gifts, Box 1, William Bingham Correspondence, Edmund S. Muskie Archives & Special Collections, Bates College, Lewiston, Maine.

307. Letter, William Bingham II to Dr. Clifton D. Gray, November 24, 1923, Assistant to the President, Series II, Wills & Gifts, Box 1, William Bingham Correspondence, Edmund S. Muskie Archives & Special Collections, Bates College, Lewiston, Maine.

308. Letter, John G. Gehring to Dr. Clifton D. Gray, May 15, 1924, Assistant to the President, Series II, Wills & Gifts, Box 1, William Bingham Correspondence, Edmund S. Muskie Archives & Special Collections, Bates College, Lewiston, Maine.

309. Ibid.

310. *The Bates Student*, October 2, 1925.

311. Ibid.

312. Ibid.

313. Ibid.

314. Ibid.

315. Ibid.

316. Ibid.

317. Letter, William Bingham II to Clifton D. Gray, October 31, 1925, Assistant to the President, Series II, Wills & Gifts, Box 1, William Bingham Correspondence, Edmund S. Muskie Archives & Special Collections, Bates College, Lewiston, Maine.

318. Letter, Clifton D. Gray to William Bingham II, November 5, 1925, Assistant to the President, Series II, Wills & Gifts, Box 1, William Bingham Correspondence, Edmund S. Muskie Archives & Special Collections, Bates College, Lewiston, Maine.

319. Letter, William Bingham II to Clifton D. Gray, November 27,1925, Assistant to the President, Series II, Wills & Gifts, Box 1, William Bingham Correspondence, Edmund S. Muskie Archives & Special Collections, Bates College, Lewiston, Maine.

320. Letter, Clifton D. Gray to William Bingham II, November 8, 1925, Assistant to the President, Series II, Wills & Gifts, Box 1,

William Bingham Correspondence, Edmund S. Muskie Archives & Special Collections, Bates College, Lewiston, Maine.

321. Letter, Maria E. Pease to Clifton D. Gray, December 29,1925, , Assistant to the President, Series II, Wills & Gifts, Box 1, William Bingham Correspondence, Edmund S. Muskie Archives & Special Collections, Bates College, Lewiston, Maine.

322. For the background, see Brooks Mather Kelley, *Yale: A History* (New Haven and London: Yale University Press, 1974), pp. 22, 127.

323. See William Ganson Rose, *Cleveland: The Making of a City* (Cleveland and New York: World Publishing Company, 1950), p. 845. Will Bingham's sister, Frances Payne Bolton, also funded an addition to the Charles William Bingham Mechanical Building in 1940.

324. See Herbert Black, *Doctor, Teacher, Hospital Chief: The New England Medical Center* (Chester, Connecticut: The Globe Pequot Press, 1982), p. 52. According to Dr. Proger, who treated her in her last illness, she greatly admired the British royal family and wondered if her anxiety over Edward VIII's abdication negatively affected her health.

325. See her obituary, *The Oxford County Citizen*, December 24, 1936

326. *The Morning Press*, Santa Barbara, March 3, 1932.

327. Ibid.

Chapter 3: Life under "King George"

328. Parkman, *The Gould Academy Story*, pp. 108-109.

329. Black, *Doctor& Teacher, Hospital Chief*, p. 52.

330. Quoted in Parkman, *The Gould Academy Story*, p. 128.

331. Farnsworth, George B. Letter to Kay (no last name) 14 February 1940. Manuscript Collection 4691, William Bingham II Papers. Western Reserve Historical Society, Cleveland, Ohio.

332. Ibid.

333. See Farnsworth's account of the beginnings of the B.A.F. in "The Advancement of Rural Medicine in the December 1937 issue of *The Bulletin of the Academy of Medicine of Cleveland.*

334. Ibid.

335. The concept of the B.A.F. was based on Gehring Associates, formed in 1931, by Dr. Gehring and Doctors Joseph H. Pratt and Harry Buhrmester according to Joseph E. Garland, *An Experiment in Medicine: The First Twenty Years of the Pratt Diagnostic Clinic and the New England Medical Center* (Cambridge, Massachusetts: Riverside Press, 1960), p. 8. Gehring Associates ceased to exist after the formation of Bingham Associates in 1932.

336. Ibid.

337. Many details of Dr. Joseph Pratt biography are summarized in Garland, *An Experiment in Medicine*, pp. 4-9.

338. See Garland, *An Experiment in Medicine*, p. 9 for these details. This story is also repeated in Herbert Black, *Doctor & Teacher, Hospital Chief: Dr. Samuel Proger and the New England Medical Center* (Chester, Connecticut: Globe Pequot Press, 1982), p. 63

339. Black in *Doctor & Teacher, Hospital Chief*, p. 64 gives Will's sister, Frances, full credit for this gift.

340. For details, see John J. Leane, *A History of Rumford, Maine 1774-1972* (Rumford, Maine: Rumford Publishing Company), pp. 85-86.

341. See Garland, *An Experiment in Medicine*, p. 14

342. For a discussion of this matter see Garland, *An Experiment in Medicine*, p. 15.

343. For a discussion of the Bingham Program and its effectiveness, see Black, *Doctor & Teacher, Hospital Chief*, pp. 88-94.

344. The decision to build a surgical wing is discussed in Black, *Doctor & Teacher, Hospital Chief*, pp. 95-101.

345. For the background, see Garland, *An Experiment in Medicine*, p. 35.

346. See Garland, *An Experiment in Medicine,* pages 23-28 for this description.

347. Garland, *An Experiment in Medicine,* p. 24.

348. Ibid.

349. Ibid.

350. Ibid.

351. Ibid.

352. Ibid.

353. Ibid.

354. Ibid.

355. Ibid, p. 25.

356. Ibid.

357. Ibid, p. 26.

358. Ibid, p. 27.

359. Ibid, p. 25.

360. Ibid, p. 26.

361. Ibid, p. 28.

362. See Farnsworth, George B. Letter to Ida Bates Goff 8 November 1939. Manuscript Collection 4691, William Bingham II Papers. Western Reserve Historical Society, Cleveland, Ohio.

363. See Farnsworth, George B. Letter to Sidney Davidson 30 November 1939. Manuscript Collection 4691, William Bingham II Papers. Western Reserve Historical Society, Cleveland, Ohio.

364. Farnsworth, George B. Letter to Edmund Finnegan 9 December 1939. Manuscript Collection 4691, William Bingham II Papers. Western Reserve Historical Society, Cleveland, Ohio.

365. Farnsworth, George B. Letter to Ida Bates Goff 11 December 1939. Manuscript Collection 4691, William Bingham II Papers. Western Reserve Historical Society, Cleveland, Ohio.

366. Farnsworth, George B. Letter to Leon Jameson, M.D. 8 January 1940. Manuscript Collection 4691, William Bingham II Papers. Western Reserve Historical Society, Cleveland, Ohio.

367. See A. Russell Buchanan, *The United States and World War II,* Volume II (New York: Harper & Row, 1964), pp. 316-317.

368. Farnsworth, George B. Letter to E. W. Millett 21 October 1940. Manuscript Collection 4691, William Bingham II Papers. Western Reserve Historical Society, Cleveland, Ohio.

369. Bingham, William II. Letter to Dudley Blossom 19 November 1934. Manuscript Collection 4691, William Bingham II Papers. Western Reserve Historical Society, Cleveland, Ohio.

370. Farnsworth, George B. Letter to Opportunity Farm 11 August 1938. Manuscript Collection 4691, William Bingham II Papers. Western Reserve Historical Society, Cleveland, Ohio.

371. See handwritten note by William Bingham II on a letter dated 28 June 1938. Manuscript Collection 4691, William Bingham II Papers. Western Reserve Historical Society, Cleveland, Ohio.

372. Farnsworth, George B. Letter to June H. Hunter 24 August 1939. Manuscript Collection 4691, William Bingham II Papers. Western Reserve Historical Society, Cleveland, Ohio.

373. Bingham, William II. Letter to George B. Farnsworth 5 October 1937. Manuscript Collection 4691, William Bingham II Papers. Western Reserve Historical Society, Cleveland, Ohio.

374. Bingham, William II. Letter to George B. Farnsworth, undated. Manuscript Collection 4691, William Bingham II Papers. Western Reserve Historical Society, Cleveland, Ohio. Although undated, the letter appears to have been written about the same time as the others on this topic, presumably in October 1937.

375. Farnsworth, George B. Letter to William Bingham II 18 February 1943. Manuscript Collection 4691, William Bingham II Papers. Western Reserve Historical Society, Cleveland, Ohio.

376. Ibid.

377. Ibid.

378. Bingham, William II. Letter to June Hills Hunter, undated (ca. 1937). Manuscript Collection 4691, William Bingham II Papers. Western Reserve Historical Society, Cleveland, Ohio.

379. Hunter, June Hills. Letter to George B. Farnsworth 22 August 1939. Manuscript Collection 4691, William Bingham II Papers. Western Reserve Historical Society, Cleveland, Ohio.

380. Ibid.

381. Farnsworth, George B. Letter to June Hills Hunter 24 August 1939. Manuscript Collection 4691, William Bingham II Papers. Western Reserve Historical Society, Cleveland, Ohio.

382. Farnsworth, George B. Letter to June Hills Hunter 30 December 1939. Manuscript Collection 4691, William Bingham II Papers. Western Reserve Historical Society, Cleveland, Ohio.

383. Farnsworth, George B. Letter to June Hills Hunter 27 December 1939. Manuscript Collection 4691, William Bingham II Papers. Western Reserve Historical Society, Cleveland, Ohio.

384. Farnsworth, George B. Letter to June Hunter Hills 27 March 1939. Manuscript Collection 4691, William Bingham II Papers. Western Reserve Historical Society, Cleveland, Ohio.

385. Farnsworth, George B. Letter to June Hunter Hills 27 March 1939. Manuscript Collection 4691, William Bingham II Papers. Western Reserve Historical Society, Cleveland, Ohio.

386. Bingham, William II. Memo to George B. Farnsworth 21 April 1937. Manuscript Collection 4691, William Bingham II Papers. Western Reserve Historical Society, Cleveland, Ohio.

387. Ibid.

388. Bingham, William II. Memo to George Farnsworth 19 February 1937. Manuscript Collection 4691, William Bingham II Papers. Western Reserve Historical Society, Cleveland, Ohio.

389. Ibid.

390. Ibid.

391. Ibid.

392. Homer E. Lawrence, M.D., was an Ohio native, graduate of Oberlin and Harvard Medical School, spent some time at the Pratt Diagnostic Hospital before taking up the Gould Academy position. See *Oxford County Citizen*, February 6, 1941.

393. Hunter, June Hills. Letter to George B. Farnsworth 10 October 1941. Manuscript Collection 4691, William Bingham II Papers. Western Reserve Historical Society, Cleveland, Ohio.

394. Hunter, June Hills. Letter to George B. Farnsworth 29 January 1938. Manuscript Collection 4691, William Bingham II Papers. Western Reserve Historical Society, Cleveland, Ohio.

395. Hunter, June Hills. Letter to George B. Farnsworth 29 January 1938. Manuscript Collection 4691, William Bingham II Papers. Western Reserve Historical Society, Cleveland, Ohio.

396. See Leane, *A History of Rumford, Maine 1774-1972*, pp. 65-66.

397. Hunter, June Hills. Letter to George B. Farnsworth 13 May 1936. Manuscript Collection 4691, William Bingham II Papers. Western Reserve Historical Society, Cleveland, Ohio.

398. Hand-written note attached to letter cited above.

399. Hunter, June Hills. Letter to George B. Farnsworth July 1936. Manuscript Collection 4691, William Bingham II Papers. Western Reserve Historical Society, Cleveland, Ohio.

400. *The Oxford County Citizen*, June 1, 1952.

401. *The Oxford County Citizen,* July 9, 1959. The 1959 *Bethel Town Report* listed her age as 75, but the author's grandmother, Edith K. Howe, who served as her housekeeper for two years, stated that she believed Betty was in her nineties at the time of death. Her husband was eighty-seven when he died seven years earlier.

402. *The Oxford County Citizen*, July 9, 1959.

403. *The Oxford County Citizen*, July 9, 1959

404. Farnsworth, George B. Letter to Ellery C. Park 20 October 1938. Manuscript Collection 4691, William Bingham II Papers. Western Reserve Historical Society, Cleveland, Ohio.

405. Ibid.

406. See note 363 above. After his mother's death in December 1936, Dr. Farnsworth set up some kind of trust to benefit, in his words, "the faithful Thurstons [Guy and Betty Burns]," who he declared are "nicely set for their old age." It is not clear if the funds came from Will Bingham or from Marian True Gehring's estate.

407. Dr. Farnsworth was apparently so impressed with Mrs. Thurston's competency that he noted in a letter to her that he

lamented the pay disparity between men and women. He also was periodically able to provide her with confidential information, for example, that Will was making the gift of an electric organ to the Bethel Congregational Church, where she was a member. See Farnsworth, George B. Letter to Betty Burns Thurston 7 May 1941. Manuscript Collection 4691, William Bingham II Papers. Western Reserve Historical Society, Cleveland, Ohio.

408. Farnsworth, George B. Letter to Betty Burns Thurston 6 July 1944. Manuscript Collection 4691, William Bingham II Papers. Western Reserve Historical Society, Cleveland, Ohio.

409. Challenge to Will of Guy L. Thurston, Sr., by Guy L. Thurston, Jr., Bertha Charick and Gerry Brooks, their Attorney of Record, Oxford County Probate Court, South Paris, Maine, October 1952.

410. Ibid.

411. Ibid.

412. Ibid.

413. Ibid.

414. Ibid.

415. Farnsworth, George B. Letter to Mrs. George H. Benn, ca. November 1938. Manuscript Collection 4691, William Bingham II Papers. Western Reserve Historical Society, Cleveland, Ohio.

416. Ibid.

417. Farnsworth, George B. Letter to _____ Nickerson July 1938. Manuscript Collection 4691, William Bingham II Papers. Western Reserve Historical Society, Cleveland, Ohio.

418. Farnsworth, George B. Letter to John F. Pollard 19 April 19, 1938. Manuscript Collection 4691, William Bingham II Papers. Western Reserve Historical Society, Cleveland, Ohio.

419. Ibid.

420. Ibid.

421. Ibid.

422. Farnsworth, George B. Letter to Lindsay Lord 13 November 1938. Manuscript Collection 4691, William Bingham II Papers. Western Reserve Historical Society, Cleveland, Ohio.

423. Ibid.

424. Farnsworth, George B. Letter to Bert L. Bryant, M.D., 22 May 1937. Manuscript Collection 4691, William Bingham II Papers. Western Reserve Historical Society, Cleveland, Ohio.

425. Ibid.

426. See note 382 above. There is evidence that Will Bingham may have occupied one of the "Lendy Houses" whenever he visited Christmas Cove with Dr. Farnsworth.

427. Ireland, Elwood. Letter to George B. Farnsworth 25 January 1943. Manuscript Collection 4691, William Bingham II Papers. Western Reserve Historical Society, Cleveland, Ohio.

428. Ibid.

429. Lockwood, Helen E. Letter to George B. Farnsworth 9 February 1944. Manuscript Collection 4691, William Bingham II Papers. Western Reserve Historical Society, Cleveland, Ohio.

430. "Freshman." Letter to George B. Farnsworth 3 February 1944. Manuscript Collection 4691, William Bingham II Papers. Western Reserve Historical Society, Cleveland, Ohio.

431. Lockwood, Helen E. Letter to George B. Farnsworth 22 May 22, 1944. Manuscript Collection 4691, William Bingham II Papers. Western Reserve Historical Society, Cleveland, Ohio.

432. Riggs, Margaret. Letter to Muriel Cox 22 June 1944. Manuscript Collection 4691, William Bingham II Papers. Western Reserve Historical Society, Cleveland, Ohio.

433. Ibid.

434. Ibid.

435. Farnsworth, George B. Letter to "Freshman" 25 June 1943. Manuscript Collection 4691, William Bingham II Papers. Western Reserve Historical Society, Cleveland, Ohio.

436. Ibid.

437. Ibid.

438. Farnsworth, George B. Letter to Margaret Riggs 25 June 1944. Manuscript Collection 4691, William Bingham II Papers. Western Reserve Historical Society, Cleveland, Ohio.

439. Ibid.

440. Farnsworth, George B. Letter to Helen Lockwood 18 May 1944. Manuscript Collection 4691, William Bingham II Papers. Western Reserve Historical Society, Cleveland, Ohio.

441. Farnsworth, George B. Letter to Dr. Helen McInstry, no date, but in a folder labeled "1939." Payne Family Archives, Cleveland, Ohio, William Bingham II Correspondence, Folder: "1924-25, 1939, 1941-1951."

442. Ibid.

443. Ibid.

444. Farnsworth, George B. Letter to Virginia Louise Brown 16 August 1943. Manuscript Collection 4691, William Bingham II Papers. Western Reserve Historical Society, Cleveland, Ohio.

445. Farnsworth, George B. Letter to Virginia Louise Brown 20 August 1945. Manuscript Collection 4691, William Bingham II Papers. Western Reserve Historical Society, Cleveland, Ohio.

446. Ibid.

447. Ibid.

448. Farnsworth, George B. Letter to Betty Price 23 March 1943. Manuscript Collection 4691, William Bingham II Papers. Western Reserve Historical Society, Cleveland, Ohio.

449. Ibid.

450. Farnsworth, George B. Letter to Betty Price 10 July 1944. Manuscript Collection 4691, William Bingham II Papers. Western Reserve Historical Society, Cleveland, Ohio.

451. For some of the background in this case, see Farnsworth, George B. Letter to Percy Crane 3 March 1941. Manuscript Collection 4691, William Bingham II Papers. Western Reserve Historical Society, Cleveland, Ohio. Percy Crane, who had once been an administrator at Gould Academy, was the Registrar at the

University of Maine. Dr. Farnsworth asked Crane to keep an eye on Than.

452. Farnsworth, George B. Letter to Than Bartholomaei 23 August 1941. Manuscript Collection 4691, William Bingham II Papers. Western Reserve Historical Society, Cleveland, Ohio.

453. Ibid.

454. Ibid.

455. Ibid.

456. Farnsworth, George B. Letter to Natalie Bartholomaei 20 August 1941. Manuscript Collection 4691, William Bingham II Papers. Western Reserve Historical Society, Cleveland, Ohio.

457. Ibid.

458. Ibid.

459. Aveson, Ruth. Letter to George B. Farnsworth 4 March 1942. Manuscript Collection 4691, William Bingham II Papers. Western Reserve Historical Society, Cleveland, Ohio.

460. Farnsworth, George B. Letter to Ruth Aveson 10 March 1942. Manuscript Collection 4691, William Bingham II Papers. Western Reserve Historical Society, Cleveland, Ohio.

461. Bingham, William II. Memo to Neal Dale 19 September 1940. Manuscript Collection 4691, William Bingham II Papers. Western Reserve Historical Society, Cleveland, Ohio.

462. Farnsworth, George B. Letter to Nettie Hastings Chapman 1 November 1937. Manuscript Collection 4691, William Bingham II Papers. Western Reserve Historical Society, Cleveland, Ohio.

463. Farnsworth, George B. Letter to John Chasson 19 October 1939. Manuscript Collection 4691, William Bingham II Papers. Western Reserve Historical Society, Cleveland, Ohio.

464. Ibid.

465. Bingham, William II. Memo to George B. Farnsworth 11 September 1944. Manuscript Collection 4691, William Bingham II Papers. Western Reserve Historical Society, Cleveland, Ohio.

466. Hunter, June Hills. Letter to George B. Farnsworth 28 September 1944. Manuscript Collection 4691, William Bingham II Papers. Western Reserve Historical Society, Cleveland, Ohio.

467. Ibid.

468. Farnsworth, George B. Letter to Deputy Sheriff John Johnson 4 December 1944. Manuscript Collection 4691, William Bingham II Papers. Western Reserve Historical Society, Cleveland, Ohio.

469. Ibid.

470. Farnsworth, George B. Letter to Robert Chandler 15 August 1945. Manuscript Collection 4691, William Bingham II Papers. Western Reserve Historical Society, Cleveland, Ohio.

471. Ibid.

472. Farnsworth, George B. Letter to John Chapitis 26 February 1939. Manuscript Collection 4691, William Bingham II Papers. Western Reserve Historical Society, Cleveland, Ohio.

473. Memoir submitted to the Bethel Historical Society by Daniel F. Hanley, M.D., December 1997. Collections of the Bethel Historical Society, Bethel, Maine.

474. Farnsworth, George B. Letter to Ida Lee Clough 19 August 1946. Manuscript Collection 4691, William Bingham II Papers. Western Reserve Historical Society, Cleveland, Ohio.

475. Ibid.

476. Farnsworth, George B. Letter to Mary Clough 11 November 1940. Manuscript Collection 4691, William Bingham II Papers. Western Reserve Historical Society, Cleveland, Ohio.

477. Farnsworth, George B. Letter to Elizabeth Melville 4 September 1941. Manuscript Collection 4691, William Bingham II Papers. Western Reserve Historical Society, Cleveland, Ohio.

478. Farnsworth, George B. Letter to Mrs. Richard Jeffrey 16 May 1938. Manuscript Collection 4691, William Bingham II Papers. Western Reserve Historical Society, Cleveland, Ohio.

479. See note 399, above.

480. Farnsworth, George B. Letter to Bernice Spearin 23 February 1941. Manuscript Collection 4691, William Bingham II Papers. Western Reserve Historical Society, Cleveland, Ohio.

481. Ibid.

482. Ibid.

483. Farnsworth, George B. Letter to Harry Wilson, M.D., 6 January 1941. Manuscript Collection 4691, William Bingham II Papers. Western Reserve Historical Society, Cleveland, Ohio.

484. Ibid.

485. Ibid.

486. Ibid.

487. Ibid.

488. Ibid.

489. Farnsworth, George B. Undated letter to Dr. Lawrence W. Baker. Manuscript Collection 4691, William Bingham II Papers. Western Reserve Historical Society, Cleveland, Ohio.

490. Ibid.

491. Ibid.

492. Ibid.

493. Bingham, William II. Memo to George B. Farnsworth 17 July 1937. Manuscript Collection 4691, William Bingham II Papers. Western Reserve Historical Society, Cleveland, Ohio.

494. Farnsworth, George B. Letter to William Bingham II 17 October 1937. Manuscript Collection 4691, William Bingham II Papers. Western Reserve Historical Society, Cleveland, Ohio.

495. Farnsworth, George B. Letter to Bert (Bryant) 29 May 1939. Manuscript Collection 4691, William Bingham II Papers. Western Reserve Historical Society, Cleveland, Ohio.

496. See Bingham note on letter from Julia Raines to William Bingham II 27 April 1937. Manuscript Collection 4691, William Bingham II Papers. Western Reserve Historical Society, Cleveland, Ohio.

497. See William Ganson Rose, *Cleveland: The Making of a City* (Cleveland: World Publishing Company, 1950), p. 845, for a concise discussion of this building.

498. Note on letter from Frank A. Inail to William Bingham II 29 August 1939. Manuscript Collection 4691, William Bingham II Papers. Western Reserve Historical Society, Cleveland, Ohio.

499. Bingham, William II. Memo to George B. Farnsworth 10 October 1936. Manuscript Collection 4691, William Bingham II Papers. Western Reserve Historical Society, Cleveland, Ohio.

500. See directive to pay $10,000 from the Bingham account of U.S. Trust 1 January 1951. Manuscript Collection 4691, William Bingham II Papers. Western Reserve Historical Society, Cleveland, Ohio.

501. Farnsworth, George B. Undated (1936) memo to William Bingham II. Manuscript Collection 4691, William Bingham II Papers. Western Reserve Historical Society, Cleveland, Ohio.

502. Ibid.

503. Ibid.

504. See Bingham note on memo from George B. Farnsworth to William Bingham II 13 November 1942. Manuscript Collection 4691, William Bingham II Papers. Western Reserve Historical Society, Cleveland, Ohio.

505. Ibid.

506. Farnsworth, George B. Letter to Bryan Hanks 1 December 1940. Manuscript Collection 4691, William Bingham II Papers. Western Reserve Historical Society, Cleveland, Ohio. And Bingham, William II. Letter to Hebron Sanitarium 30 July 1941. Manuscript Collection 4691, William Bingham II Papers. Western Reserve Historical Society, Cleveland, Ohio.

507. Farnsworth, George B. Letter to Haywood Burton October 1937. Manuscript Collection 4691, William Bingham II Papers. Western Reserve Historical Society, Cleveland, Ohio.

508. Ibid.

509. Ibid.

510. Farnsworth, George B. Letter to Mrs. Scott Robertson 18 April 1936. Manuscript Collection 4691, William Bingham II Papers. Western Reserve Historical Society, Cleveland, Ohio.

511. Ibid.

512. Ibid.

513. Farnsworth, George B. Letter to Donald Partridge 20 January 1940. Manuscript Collection 4691, William Bingham II Papers. Western Reserve Historical Society, Cleveland, Ohio.

514. Bingham, William II. Note to Donald Partridge 19 January 1940. Manuscript Collection 4691, William Bingham II Papers. Western Reserve Historical Society, Cleveland, Ohio.

515. Farnsworth, George B. Letter to James C. Oliver 16 December 1939. Manuscript Collection 4691, William Bingham II Papers. Western Reserve Historical Society, Cleveland, Ohio.

516. Farnsworth, George B. Letter to Mrs. Eugene Norton 18 March 1939. Manuscript Collection 4691, William Bingham II Papers. Western Reserve Historical Society, Cleveland, Ohio.

517. Ibid.

518. See *Oxford County Citizen*, June 3, 1937, and Randall H. Bennett, *Oxford County, Maine: A Guide to Its Historic Architecture* (Bethel, Maine: Oxford County Historic Resource Survey, 1984), pp. 35-36.

519. Farnsworth, George B. Letter to Alfred Whitman 4 April 1938. Manuscript Collection 4691, William Bingham II Papers. Western Reserve Historical Society, Cleveland, Ohio.

520. Farnsworth, George B. Letter to Edward Hume, M.D., 27 April 1939. Manuscript Collection 4691, William Bingham II Papers. Western Reserve Historical Society, Cleveland, Ohio.

521. Ibid.

522. Ibid.

523. Farnsworth, George B. Letter to Franklin W. Johnson 1938. Manuscript Collection 4691, William Bingham II Papers. Western Reserve Historical Society, Cleveland, Ohio.

524. Farnsworth, George B. Letter to Mr. Higgins 31 December 1937. Manuscript Collection 4691, William Bingham II Papers. Western Reserve Historical Society, Cleveland, Ohio.

525. Ibid.

526. Ibid.

527. Farnsworth, George B. Letter to Miss Cryan 9 December 1937. Manuscript Collection 4691, William Bingham II Papers. Western Reserve Historical Society, Cleveland, Ohio.

528. Farnsworth, George B. Letter to Dr. A. S. Degg, Boston University School of Medicine, 13 May 1939. Manuscript Collection 4691, William Bingham II Papers. Western Reserve Historical Society, Cleveland, Ohio.

529. Farnsworth, George B. Letter to Emile Cote 2 August 1939. Manuscript Collection 4691, William Bingham II Papers. Western Reserve Historical Society, Cleveland, Ohio.

530. Farnsworth, George B. Letter to Dean Henry H. Meyer 30 November 1939. Manuscript Collection 4691, William Bingham II Papers. Western Reserve Historical Society, Cleveland, Ohio.

531. Bingham, William II. Memo to George B. Farnsworth 20 December 1934. Manuscript Collection 4691, William Bingham II Papers. Western Reserve Historical Society, Cleveland, Ohio.

532. Ibid.

533. Farnsworth, George B. Letter to Dr. David Fairchild 29 October 1943. Manuscript Collection 4691, William Bingham II Papers. Western Reserve Historical Society, Cleveland, Ohio.

534. Ibid.

535. Ibid.

536. Ibid.

537. Ibid.

538. Holt, Hamilton. Telegram to William Bingham II 22 May 1940. Manuscript Collection 4691, William Bingham II Papers. Western Reserve Historical Society, Cleveland, Ohio.

539. Farnsworth, George B. Letter to Hamilton Holt 24 April 1942. Manuscript Collection 4691, William Bingham II Papers. Western Reserve Historical Society, Cleveland, Ohio.

540. Farnsworth, George B. Letter to E. C. Park 31 December 1938. Manuscript Collection 4691, William Bingham II Papers. Western Reserve Historical Society, Cleveland, Ohio. Park came to Bethel from the Oxford Hills area and attended Hebron Academy, as did Waterman.

541. Waterman, Charles. Letter to George B. Farnsworth 8 January 1939. Manuscript Collection 4691, William Bingham II Papers. Western Reserve Historical Society, Cleveland, Ohio.

542. See note 371, above. In 1940, Will also sent $375 to Langbourne W. Williams, Jr., Chairman of the Finance Committee, Democrats for Wilkie. Bingham, William II. Letter to L. W. Williams, Jr., 28 October 1940. Manuscript Collection 4691, William Bingham II Papers. Western Reserve Historical Society, Cleveland, Ohio.

543. Ibid.

544. Waterman, Charles. Letter to William Bingham II 1938. Manuscript Collection 4691, William Bingham II Papers. Western Reserve Historical Society, Cleveland, Ohio.

545. Farnsworth, George B. Letter to William Bingham II 21 July 1939. Manuscript Collection 4691, William Bingham II Papers. Western Reserve Historical Society, Cleveland, Ohio.

546. Waterman, Charles. Undated letter (ca. December 1938) to William Bingham II. Manuscript Collection 4691, William Bingham II Papers. Western Reserve Historical Society, Cleveland, Ohio.

547. Farnsworth, George B. Letter to William Bingham II 30 November 1942. Manuscript Collection 4691, William Bingham II Papers. Western Reserve Historical Society, Cleveland, Ohio.

548. Ibid.

549. Farnsworth, George B. Memo to William Bingham II 2 January 1940. Manuscript Collection 4691, William Bingham II Papers. Western Reserve Historical Society, Cleveland, Ohio.

550. Farnsworth, George B. Letter to William Bingham II 25 January 1939. Manuscript Collection 4691, William Bingham II Papers. Western Reserve Historical Society, Cleveland, Ohio.

551. Ibid.

552. Ibid.

553. Farnsworth, George B. Letter to William Bingham II 4 February 1943. Manuscript Collection 4691, William Bingham II Papers. Western Reserve Historical Society, Cleveland, Ohio.

554. Davidson, Sidney. Letter to George Farnsworth 19 January 1942. Manuscript Collection 4691, William Bingham II Papers. Western Reserve Historical Society, Cleveland, Ohio.

555. Davidson, Sidney. Undated letter (ca. January 1946) to George Farnsworth. Manuscript Collection 4691, William Bingham II Papers. Western Reserve Historical Society, Cleveland, Ohio.

556. Farnsworth, George B. Note to William Bingham II 18 January 1946. Manuscript Collection 4691, William Bingham II Papers. Western Reserve Historical Society, Cleveland, Ohio.

557. Farnsworth, George B. Letter to Sidney Davidson 24 January 1946. Manuscript Collection 4691, William Bingham II Papers. Western Reserve Historical Society, Cleveland, Ohio.

558. Ibid.

559. Ibid.

560. Ibid.

561. Farnsworth, George B. Letter to Joseph Barr 24 January 1946. Manuscript Collection 4691, William Bingham II Papers. Western Reserve Historical Society, Cleveland, Ohio.

562. Ibid.

563. *Advertiser-Democrat*, March 24, 1939.

564. Undated notes (probably November 1938) by William Bingham II and George B. Farnsworth. Manuscript Collection 4691, William Bingham II Papers. Western Reserve Historical Society, Cleveland, Ohio.

565. Farnsworth, George B. Letter to Sidney Davidson 24 November 1938. Manuscript Collection 4691, William Bingham II Papers. Western Reserve Historical Society, Cleveland, Ohio.

566. Farnsworth, George B. Letter to Sidney Davidson 17 December 1946. Manuscript Collection 4691, William Bingham II Papers. Western Reserve Historical Society, Cleveland, Ohio.

567. For the toboggan slide, see reference to it in a letter from A. M. Weeks to William Bingham II 29 November 1914. Manuscript Collection 4691, William Bingham II Papers. Western Reserve Historical Society, Cleveland, Ohio. For the Bethel Inn tennis courts and golf course, see *The Oxford County Citizen,* June 17, 1915, and for the theater, *The Oxford County Citizen,* November 25, 1915.

568. The Oxford County Citizen, July 25, 1929.

569. See note 393 above.

570. *The Oxford County Citizen*, December 29, 1932.

571. A set of proposed plans are in the Collections of the Bethel Historical Society, Bethel, Maine.

572. *The Oxford County Citizen*, October 30, 1941.

573. Farnsworth, George B. Letter to William Bingham II 15 July 1941. Manuscript Collection 4691, William Bingham II Papers. Western Reserve Historical Society, Cleveland, Ohio.

574. For information on Brewster's close association with Senator McCarthy, see Thomas C. Reeves, *The Life and Times of Joe McCarthy: A Biography* (London: Blond & Briggs, 1982), pp. 345, 388, 418. Brewster would later serve with the first woman elected to the U.S. Senate, Margaret Chase Smith, who in 1950 delivered her "Declaration of Conscience" speech on the U.S. Senate floor, where she denounced McCarthy's demagogic, "big lie" tactics. Mrs. Smith was elected in 1940 to the House of Representatives to replace her late husband, Clyde Smith—the same year Will Bingham's sister, Frances Payne Bolton, was elected to assume her deceased husband's, Chester Bolton's, seat representing Ohio in the U.S. House. Mrs. Smith and Mrs. Bolton became lifelong friends.

Senator Brewster also persuaded Dr. Farnsworth to sponsor a Kingfield, Maine, resident to attend Gould Academy, who later ran away and otherwise failed to distinguish himself. See Farnsworth, George B. Letter to Ralph Owen Brewster 20 January 1941. Manuscript Collection 4691, William Bingham II Papers. Western Reserve Historical Society, Cleveland, Ohio.

575. Ibid.

576. Ibid.

577. Ibid.

578. Farnsworth, George B. Letter to William Bingham II 15 July 1941. Manuscript Collection 4691, William Bingham II Papers. Western Reserve Historical Society, Cleveland, Ohio.

579. Farnsworth, George B. Letter to Hugh S. Kelley 3 October 1941. Manuscript Collection 4691, William Bingham II Papers. Western Reserve Historical Society, Cleveland, Ohio.

580. Ibid.

581. Kelley, Hugh S. Letter to George B. Farnsworth 5 June 1942. Manuscript Collection 4691, William Bingham II Papers. Western Reserve Historical Society, Cleveland, Ohio.

582. Ibid.

583. Ibid.

584. Farnsworth, George B. Letter to William Bingham II 11 November 1940. Manuscript Collection 4691, William Bingham II Papers. Western Reserve Historical Society, Cleveland, Ohio.

585. Anderson, George, DDS. Letter to George B. Farnsworth 12 May 1942. Manuscript Collection 4691, William Bingham II Papers. Western Reserve Historical Society, Cleveland, Ohio. Dr. Farnsworth also complained in one instance that Dr. Anderson had substituted his son for a dental assistant. Farnsworth, George B. Letter to George J. Anderson, DDS, 23 December 1940. Manuscript Collection 4691, William Bingham II Papers. Western Reserve Historical Society, Cleveland, Ohio.

586. Letter, Edwin Gehring, M.D., to Norman Gehring, M.D., September 5, 1949, Collections of the Bethel Historical Society, Bethel, Maine, Box 21, Folder: "Gehring."

587. Numbers for Dr. Farnsworth's compensation for overseeing Will's affairs are not clear. For the years 1940-43, it was listed at $58,870 annually plus expenses, which may also have included retirement and survivor's benefits. Farnsworth, George B. Memo to William Bingham II 2 February 1943. Manuscript Collection 4691, William Bingham II Papers. Western Reserve Historical Society, Cleveland, Ohio.

588. Will was so impressed by the Maine General Hospital under Edwin Gehring's direction that he was willing to give $20,000 to that institution, noting that he could not "believe anything better could be done with that amount of money." Bingham, William II. Memo to George B. Farnsworth 29 March 1934. Manuscript Collection 4691, William Bingham II Papers. Western Reserve Historical Society, Cleveland, Ohio.

Chapter 4: Life with Dr. Walters

589. Much of this biographical information is from Eva M. Bean. See "Eva Bean Papers," Box 11, Collections of the Bethel Historical Society, Bethel, Maine. Obituary, *The Oxford County Citizen,* February 2, 1961. Several emails received by the author in February and March of 2013 from Walter's two grandsons, Kirk and Peter McWilliams, also contain information about their grandparents.

590. Walters, Dr. Arthur. Letter to Sidney W. Davidson 10 April 1948. Manuscript Collection 4691, William Bingham II Papers. Western Reserve Historical Society, Cleveland, Ohio.

591. Walters, Dr. Arthur. Letter to Dr. David Fairchild 9 June 1947. Manuscript Collection 4691, William Bingham II Papers. Western Reserve Historical Society, Cleveland, Ohio.

592. Ibid.

593. Ibid.

594. Ibid.

595. Ibid.

596. See *Bowdoin Orient*, February 13, 2009, for account of an exhibit of this 1942 gift to Bowdoin College.

597. Walters, Dr. Arthur L. Letter to Sidney Davidson 5 May 1954. Manuscript Collection 4691, William Bingham II Papers. Western Reserve Historical Society, Cleveland, Ohio.

598. Ernest C. Mariner, *The History of Colby College* (Waterville, ME: Colby College Press, 1963), p. 396.

599. Davidson, Sidney W. Letter to Robert Gleason 29 June 1950. Manuscript Collection 4691, William Bingham II Papers. Western Reserve Historical Society, Cleveland, Ohio.

600. Farnsworth, George B. Letter to J. Seelye Bixler 21 October 1944. Manuscript Collection 4691, William Bingham II Papers. Western Reserve Historical Society, Cleveland, Ohio.

601. Ibid.

602. Ibid.

603. Ibid.

604. Ibid.

605. Ibid. The reference to the "heavy load" borne by J. Seelye Bixler was the decision to move the campus from downtown Waterville to Mayflower Hill a mile away.

606. Bixler, J. Seelye. Letter to George B. Farnsworth 20 April 1943. Manuscript Collection 4691, William Bingham II Papers. Western Reserve Historical Society, Cleveland, Ohio.

607. Farnsworth, George B. Letter to Franklin Johnson 1 November 1940. Manuscript Collection 4691, William Bingham II Papers. Western Reserve Historical Society, Cleveland, Ohio.

608. Farnsworth, George B. Letter to E. W. Millett 21 October 1940. Manuscript Collection 4691, William Bingham II Papers. Western Reserve Historical Society, Cleveland, Ohio.

609. Ibid.

610. For a description of the building, see Patricia McGraw Anderson, *The Architecture of Bowdoin College* (Brunswick, Maine: Bowdoin College Museum of Art, 1988), pp. 109-110.

611. Palmer, Harry. Letter to Dr. Arthur Walters 2 May 1952. Manuscript Collection 4691, William Bingham II Papers. Western Reserve Historical Society, Cleveland, Ohio.

612. Ibid.

613. Sills, Kenneth. Letter to William Bingham II 7 September 1949. Manuscript Collection 4691, William Bingham II Papers. Western Reserve Historical Society, Cleveland, Ohio.

614. Davidson, Sidney. Letter to Dr. Arthur Walters 18 April 1949. Manuscript Collection 4691, William Bingham II Papers. Western Reserve Historical Society, Cleveland, Ohio.

615. Ibid.

616. Ibid.

617. Walters, Arthur, M.D. Letter to Dr. David Fairchild 30 June 1953. Manuscript Collection 4691, William Bingham II Papers. Western Reserve Historical Society, Cleveland, Ohio.

618. Email, John P. Howe III, M.D., to the author, 21 April 2013.

619. Email, Peter A. McWilliams to the author, 6 March 2013.

620. Ibid.

621. Ibid.

622. Ibid.

623. Walters, Arthur. Letter to Betty Burns Thurston 19 February 1955. Manuscript Collection 4691, William Bingham II Papers. Western Reserve Historical Society, Cleveland, Ohio.

624. Thurston, Betty Burns. Letter to Arthur Walters 28 February 1955. Manuscript Collection 4691, William Bingham II Papers. Western Reserve Historical Society, Cleveland, Ohio.

625. *The Oxford County Citizen*, June 16, 1955.

626. *The Oxford County Citizen*, June 14, 1956.

627. Herbert Black, Doctor and Teacher, Hospital Chief: Dr. Samuel Proger and the New England Medical Center (Chester, CT: Globe Pequot Press, 1982), p. 59.

628. Ibid.

629. From Edith K. Howe's diaries (1948-1954), it is possible to gain insights into the Bingham household during the final years of his life. Mrs. Howe records his eating habits and his gain or loss of weight, as well as the comings and goings of various professionals attending to Will, including dentists, barbers and others. It is also possible to determine what Will preferred to eat: largely roasts of meat (often lamb, chicken or beef) and various vegetables, along with desserts consisting of cakes, pies and puddings. According to family legend, he often cautioned her to hold down household expenses, which must have been second nature to her, as she fully embodied the classic New England adage, "Use it up, wear it out, make it do or do without."

630. Apparently, Will had to rely solely on private railcar transportation, as Dr. Farnsworth noted to his assistant, Weston Poole, observing, "You know the problem he represents on an ordinary train." See Farnsworth, George B. Letter to Weston Poole 18 September 1942. Manuscript Collection 4691, William Bingham II Papers. Western Reserve Historical Society, Cleveland, Ohio.

631. Noted by Dr. Proger; see Black, *Doctor & Teacher, Hospital Chief*, p. 56.

632. Ibid.

633. Bolton, Frances P. Letter to Elizabeth Blossom 30 July 1956. Manuscript Collection 4691, William Bingham II Papers. Western Reserve Historical Society, Cleveland, Ohio.

634. Ibid.

635. Ibid.

636. This document is found in Manuscript Collection 4691, William Bingham II Papers. Western Reserve Historical Society, Cleveland, Ohio.

637. Speech of Frances P. Bolton, Member of Congress, 22nd District of Ohio, at Dedication Ceremonies of Bingham Hall at Gould Academy, Bethel, Maine, October 5, 1963. Bethel Historical Society, Gould Academy Archives, Collection 1, Box 10.

INDEX

American College of Physicians, 122

America Committee for Armenian and Syrian Relief, 52

American Relief Administration, 52

Anderson, George J. (DDS), 118

Anderson, Newton Mitchell, 10, 14, 22

Andrews, William, 32-33

Androscoggin River, 83

Anthony, Dora, 77, 113

Augusta, Maine, 138

Baker, Lawrence W. (Dr.), 101

Bangor, Maine, 70, 72

Barr, Joseph, 73, 115, 119, 127, 129-130,

Barr, Robert T., 29-30

Bartholomaei, Natalie True, 93

Bartholomaei, Nathaniel ("Nat"; "Than") True, 92-94

Bates, Guy (nurse), 28

Bates College, 33, 56-61, 65

Bates Student, The, 60

Battle of Fallen Timbers, 2

Bean, Eva, 125

Beers, Clifford, 101-102

Bell, Alexander Graham, 42

Bell, Mabel Hubbard, 42

Bellevue Hospital, 71

Bethel, Maine, 28, 31, 33-37, 41, 48, 51, 53-54, 58, 60, 67, 69-70, 81, 84-85, 99-100, 111, 114, 118-119, 125, 128, 131-133, 136-137

Bethel Academy, 31

Bethel High School, 31

Bethel Historical Society, 98

Bethel Inn, 37-40, 44-46, 53, 55, 58, 85-87, 94, 100, 110, 113-117, 132-133, 136

Bethel Inn Corporation, 43-44

Bethel League, 37-40,

Bethel Library Association, 45

Bethel Methodist Church, 104-105

Bethel Savings Bank, 45

Bethel Water Company, 53-54

Bethel Water District, 54

Bingham, Charles William (father), 4-14, 17-19, 22-25, 30, 42, 48-51, 61-62, 108, 133-134

Bingham, Cyrus (Captain), 1

Bingham, Eleazer (Dr.), 1

Bingham, Elizabeth Beardsley (sister; *see also* Blossom, Elizabeth), 3, 6, 9, 22

Bingham, Frances (sister; *see also* Bolton, Frances), 6, 9-10

Bingham, Henry ("Harry"; brother), 9, 50, 76

Bingham, Mary ("Molly") Perry Payne (mother), 7-9, 11-13, 17, 19-20, 25, 29, 53, 71, 108, 134

Bingham, Oliver Perry (brother), 9, 11-14, 17-22, 29, 108, 134

Bingham, Stephen, 1

Bingham, Stephen (Ensign), 1

Bingham, Thomas (Deacon), 1

Bingham, William (grandfather), 1-2

Bingham, William, 2nd: arrives in Bethel, 27, 31, 41-42, 45, 48; and Bethel League, 37-39, 40; birth, 4, 9; gives up Cleveland residency, 48-49; mental and physical health of, 23-25, 29-31, 41, 49, 61, 68, 70, 74-75, 84-85, 108, 126-127, 131-132, 134-135, 137; and music, 11-14, 17, 19, 30, 43, 45-46, 55, 92, 133; and outdoor recreation & sports, 10-14, 17-23, 25-26, 28-30; personality of, 74-75, 133, 135, 137; political sympathies, 6; purchases home at Bethel, 42, 55; and religion, 14, 16, 21, 57-58, 75, 103; resides with Mary True at Bethel, 42; early schooling, 9-12, 15-23; and World War I, 48, 50-52

Bingham Associates Fund for the Advancement of Rural Medicine (B.A.F.), 68-70, 78-79, 82, 123, 125, 138

Bingham Associates Fund of Massachusetts, 73-75

Bingham Betterment Fund, 126, 138

Bingham Forest Authority, 54

Bingham Hall, 137

Bingham Laboratory of Mechanical Engineering, 102

Bingham Program, 29, 72-74, 138

Bingham Trust, The, 138

Bixler, J. Seelye, 129

Blackwood, Sam, 115-116

Blossom, Dudley, 78, 133

Blossom, Elizabeth, 133

Boggs, Eva (nurse), 76, 82, 100

Bolton, Chester, 50

Bolton, Frances Payne
Bingham, 28-30, 42, 46, 50,
70-71, 132, 135-137

Bolton, Kenyon C., 133

Boston, 14-15, 21, 23-24, 32,
42-44, 55, 66, 69-73, 75,
106-108

Boston Dispensary, 69-71, 73

Boston Latin School, 23

Boston University's School of
Medicine, 107

Bowdoin College, 66-67, 96-99,
122, 128, 130-131

Boynton, Willard (Dr.), 86

Brewster, Ralph Owen (Sen.),
117-118

Brewster, William, 33

Broad Street (Bethel), 32, 34-
35, 39-40, 42, 44, 55, 65,
67, 125, 131

Brown, Eliza, 75-77

Brown, Virginia Louise, 92

Bryant, Bertram L. (Dr.), 68

Bryant, Lillian (True), 68

*Bulletin of the New England
Medical Center*, 119

Burton, Haywood, 104

Butler, Guy, 136

California Institute of Technology, 36

Canton, Maine, 88

Carter, Edward Perkins, 56

Carter family, 99

Case Library Association, 6

Case School of Applied
Science, 7, 62, 102

Case Western Reserve
University, 7

Chamberlain School, 90

Chambers, Walter B., 62

Chandler, Robert ("Bob"), 95-
96

Chapman, William Rogers, 42,
44

Chapman Brook, 53-55,

Charick, Bertha Thurston, 86

Charles W. Bingham Hall, 62

Charles W. Bingham
Mechanical Engineering
Building, 7, 62

Chase, George, 57

Chester, Nova Scotia, 27

Christmas Cove, Maine, 66, 77,
89, 92, 96-97, 111, 113, 117

Cilley, Harriette, 116

Citizens Savings & Loan
Association, 6

Citizens Savings and Trust
Company, 51

Civil War, 3-4, 32, 42

Cleveland Academy, 4

Cleveland Clinic, 32

Cleveland Community
Chest/Fund, 78, 102

Cleveland Iron Company, 5

Cleveland Manual Training
    School Company, 7
Cleveland Museum of Art, 6,
    102, 134
Cleveland Oat Meal Company,
    5
Cleveland Rolling Mill Com-
    pany, 3, 5
Cleveland, Moses, 2
Cleveland, Ohio, 2-3, 6, 8-9,
    11, 14, 16-17, 19, 21-25, 27-
    31, 42, 45-46, 48-49, 51-52,
    56, 62, 66, 68, 77, 102-103,
    113, 119, 121, 133
Cleveland Plain Dealer, 46
Clifton Daggett Gray Athletic
    Building, 61
Clough family, 99
Coit, Henry A., 14-15
Coit, Joseph, H., 15, 18
Colby College, 78, 106, 128-
    130
Cole Block, 43
Columbia Medical School, 97-
    98
Columbia University, 52
Community Chest of Dade
    County, Florida, 103
Concord, New Hampshire, 14-
    15
Connecticut Land Company, 2
Connecticut River Valley, 74
Constantinople, Turkey (see also
    Istanbul), 58

Constantinople College, 52
Coolidge and Carlson (archi-
    tects), 44, 55, 116
Cornell University Medical
    School, 122
Corson, D. Herman, 87
Costello, James (nurse), 28
Crane, Percy, 96
Culberson, Charles A., 36
Curran, Jean (Dr.), 29
Cuyahoga County Military
    Committee, 3
Dale, Neal, 77, 94, 111-112
Dale, Sally Farnsworth, 77
Damariscotta, Maine, 66, 111,
    118
David K. and Mary Arey
    Building for Life Sciences,
    128
Davidson, Sidney W., 67, 72-
    74, 76, 110-116, 119, 126-
    128, 130-131, 133
Degg, A. S., 107
"Delinda, The," 42
Dinsmore, Lillian, 86
Douglas Hill, Sebago, Maine,
    52
Dutton, Samuel T., 52, 71
East Bethel, Maine, 55, 84
Eastman, Max, 33
Ehle, Mrs. George, 36
Eli Lilly Company, 125
Emerson College, 107

Emory University Medical
    School, 71-72,
Ervin, Harold, 76
Euclid Avenue (Cleveland), 8-
    9, 27, 30,
Exeter Academy, 81
Fader, Edmund ("Ned"), 27-28
"Farnstede Manor," 66, 111
Farnsworth, George Bourne
    (Sr.), 32, 45, 65-66, 122
Farnsworth, George Bourne,
    Jr. (Dr.), 27, 51-52, 65-69,
    72-73, 76-112, 114-122,
    126-131, 135,
Farnsworth, Marian True (see
    Marian True Gehring)
Farnsworth, Ruth, 52, 77, 108,
    113,
Farnsworth Field House, 83,
    120, 129-130,
Farnsworth Scholarship, 98
Farnsworth Surgical Building,
    73-74, 121, 138
Farrar, Geraldine, 43
Faulke, Mary, 39-41,
Federal Bureau of Investiga-
    tion, 117
"Figulus," 108
Finnegan, Edmund, 76
First National Bank of Boston,
    74
Flood of 1936, 83
Florida, 14, 28, 62, 108-109,
    111, 127, 131-132, 135,

Franco-Prussian War, 4
Frank R. Greene Company, 42
Fuller, William, 40
Gehring, Edwin W. (Dr.), 119-
    123
Gehring, John George (Dr.),
    28, 31-42, 44-50, 57-59, 61-
    62, 65-68, 70, 85-86, 100,
    119-122, 126-127, 134-135,
    137
Gehring, Marian True, 28, 31-
    32, 34-35, 37-38, 40-43, 45-
    47, 49, 51, 58, 62, 65-67,
    70, 86, 89, 114, 119-120,
    122, 134,
Gehring, Norman (Dr.), 119,
    122
Gehring, Victor, 122
Gehring Associates, 70
Gehring Clinic, 27-28, 31, 33,
    35-36, 39, 41, 45-46, 49, 89,
    108, 134,
George Farnsworth Tennis
    Club, 65
Gerrish, Frederick H. (Dr.), 32,
    34
Goff, Ida Bates, 75-76,
Good Will-Hinckley, 78
Gorham, Maine, 92
Gould, Daniel (Rev.), 31
Gould's/Gould Academy, 30-
    31, 33, 45-47, 53, 56-59, 66-
    68, 78, 80, 83, 89, 91, 93,

96, 99, 106, 110, 114, 120,
122, 125-130, 133, 136-137
Gould Academy Story, The, 30
Grand Canyon, 51
Grand Trunk Railway, 51
Grant, Dana, 114-115
Grant, Ulysses, 3
Gray, Clifton D., 56-61
Great Depression, 77, 80, 110,
113
Greenwood, Maine, 114
Hale, George Ellery, 36
Hamilton, Bermuda, 10
Hammons, David, 44
Hanley, Daniel F., 96-98
Hanscom, Frank E., 47, 56-58,
110
"Harriette, The," 116
Harrison, Paul, 106
"Harrywold," 11
Harvard, 23, 31, 33, 35, 67, 96,
Harvard Medical School, 24,
66, 92, 120
Hawthorne, Julian, 8
Hawthorne, Nathaniel, 8
Hawthorne, Rose, 8
Hawthorne, Sophia, 8
Hawthorne, Una, 8
Hebron, Maine, 104
Herrick, Addison E., 53
Herrick, Robert, 36
Hitchcock, Morley, 19, 21-22
Hodgdon, Maine, 87-88
Holden, Liberty, 46

Holden Hall, 130
Hoover, Herbert, 52
Hope of the Variant, The, 35, 61
Horace Kelly Art Foundation,
6
Howe, John P. III, 131
Hubbard, Charles W., 43
Hubbard, Gardiner, 42
Hubbard, Mabel, 42
Hume, Edward (Dr.), 106
Hunter, June Hills, 78-84, 86,
95
Huntington Art and Polytech-
nic Trust, 6
Interseminary Commission for
Training for the Rural
Ministry, 103
Interstate Commerce Commis-
sion, 36
Institute for the Blind, 107
Ireland, Elwood, 89, 133
Istanbul, Turkey, 52-53, 71,
137,
Jackson Hole, Wyoming, 28
James, William, 102
Jenkins, ___, 16
Johns Hopkins University
Medical School, 56, 69, 125
Johns Hopkins University
School of Nursing, 125
Johnson, Franklin W., 106, 129
Johnson, John, 95

Joseph H. Pratt Diagnostic
  Hospital/Pratt Diagnostic
  Clinic, 69, 120-121, 126
Judson, Agnes, 25
Judson, Arthur, 25
Kelley, Hugh S., 117-118
King, Harry, 42
Lake View Cemetery, 133
Lake View Cemetery Associa-
  tion, 6
Lane, Franklin K., 36-37
Lawrence, Homer E., 83
Lawrence, Maude, 37, 39-40
Lewiston, Maine, 56, 70, 72
Locke's Mills, Maine, 114-115
Lord, Mrs. C. F., 42
Lord, Lindsay, 88
Lowell, Ralph, 126
Mack, Dale, 81-82
Maine Central Institute, 95
Maine General Hospital, 122
Maine Medical Association,
  120, 122
Maine Music Festival, 43
Maine Publicity Bureau, 136
Maine School of Commerce,
  99
Marian True Gehring Students'
  Home, 59, 120
Mary Payne Bingham Kinder-
  garten, 9
Massachusetts General
  Hospital, 70
Master of the Inn, The, 36

McCarthy, Joseph (Sen.), 117
McCarty, Eugene (Dr.), 71
McCoy, ___, 13
McCune, T. H., 11
McInstry, Helen, 91
McKim, Mead and White, 130
McWilliams, Peter, 131-132
Melville, Elizabeth, 99
Merrill, Fred B., 68
Metropolitan Opera, 43
Mexico, Maine, 94-95
Mexico High School, 95
Miami, Florida, 132-133
Miami Beach, Florida, 126
Miles Memorial Hospital, 118
Millett, E. W., 78, 130,
Mind That Found Itself, The, 101
Mitchell, ___, 17, 80
Mount Wilson Observatory, 36
National Committee for Mental
  Hygiene, 102
New Deal, 78
New England, 38, 40
New England Medical Center,
  72, 75, 126
New Haven Hopkins
  Grammar School, 4
Norway (Maine) Second
  Congregational Church,
  105
Oakland, Maine, 88
Odeon Hall, 34, 43, 45
Oliver, James C., 105
Opportunity Farm, 78

Ormond Beach, Florida, 108, 127
Ottawa Shooting Club, 26
Oxford County, Maine, 50, 78-80, 109, 136,
Oxford County United Parish, 103
Oxford Hills and Other Papers, The, 110
Palm Beach, Florida, 19, 29
Palmer, Harry, 130
Park, Ellery C., 44, 47, 50, 53, 68, 94, 109, 115, 121
Parker Cleveland Hall, 130
Parkman, Francis, 30
Partridge, Donald, 105
Pasadena, California, 36
Payne family, 1, 11
Payne, Henry B. (grandfather), 7-8
Payne, Mary Skinner Perry (grandmother), 7
Payne, Nathan Perry (uncle), 6
Payne, Oliver Hazard (uncle), 11, 30, 46, 51, 56
Pease, Maria, 61
Pels, ___ (Dr.), 95
Penley Brothers Company, 53
Perry-Payne Company, 6
Philadelphia, 75-76
Philadelphia (railroad car), 51
Piedmont Hospital, 71
Piscataquis County, Maine, 118

Portland, Maine, 32-34, 88, 99, 106, 118, 122
Portland Junior Technical College, 88
Portsmouth, New Hampshire, 104
Pratt, Joseph (Dr.), 68-71, 79, 95, 120-122
Pratt, Morris, 46
Pratt Diagnostic Hospital, 71-73
Presbyterian Hospital, 62, 70
Price, Betty, 92
Princeton University, 128
Proger, Samuel H. (Dr.), 67, 71-75, 100
Prospect Inn/Hotel, 42-43
Purdue University, 125
Rangeley, Maine, 83
Robert College, 53, 71
Rockefeller Fund, 74
Rockefeller's pond, 14
Rollins, F. S., 51
Rollins College, 33, 109
Roosevelt, Franklin, 77
Roosevelt, Theodore, 36
Rowe, A. T., 44
Rumford, Maine, 31, 71, 79-80, 83-84, 94-96, 107
Rumford Community Hospital, 69-71, 79, 86,
"Rumford Program," 71
Russell Sage College, 91

Santa Barbara, California, 11-
14, 28, 51, 62, 137
Santa Barbara Collegiate
School, 11
Santa Barbara Museum of
Natural History, 62-63
Scott, Ronald, 83
Sears, Horace S., 43-44, 114
Sebec, Maine, 128
Shattuck Anne Brune, 23
Shattuck, Frederick Cheever,
23-25
Shattuck, George Brune 23
Shattuck, George C., Jr., 14-15,
23
Shattuck, George Cheyne, 23
Sheffield Scientific School, 69
Sherman, Lula W., 37-39,
Shydler, ___, 17
Sills, Kenneth, 130-131
Songo Pond, 39-40,
St. Francis Hospital, 126
St. Paul's School, 14-18, 20-24,
27-28
Standard Tool Company, 5
Stevens, John Calvin, 106
Stokes, Frank Wilber, 128
"Stone House," 8
Taft, Robert, 117
Tetlow, Helen, 40
Thurston, Elizabeth ("Betty")
Burns, 67, 85-86, 94-95,
100, 128, 132-133
Thurston, Guy L., 85-87, 116

Thurston, Guy L., Jr., 86
Tiffany of New York, 44
Tompson, Frederick A., 33
True, Alfred, 42
True, Marian (*see* Marian True
Gehring)
True, Mary, 42, 45
True, Nathaniel Tuckerman
(Dr.), 31-33, 45, 65, 92
True, Susanna Webber Stevens,
65
Trust for Charity (*see* William
Bingham 2nd Trust for
Charity)
Tufts Medical School/New
England Medical Center,
69-71, 73, 128, 138
Tufts University, 130
Twentieth Century Club, 67
Union Club, 6
Union Trust Company, 6
United States Trust of New
York, 74
University of Berlin, 32
University of Maine, 92-93, 95-
96
University School, 9-10, 14, 16-
17, 22, 29,
University of Wooster (Ohio),
32
Upson, Nina Hodgdon, 45, 58
Upson, William J., 31, 37-41,
43-46, 48, 58
Vanderbilt, Mrs. William K., 58

W. Bingham & Company, 5

Walburger, Grant & Company, 114

Wallace, W. J. H., 11

Walters, Arthur L. (Dr.), 85-86, 103, 119, 125, 127-128, 130-133, 135

Walters, Louise Bitting, 125

Wampum Coal & Iron Company, 5,

Waterman, Charles, 109-110

West Palm Beach, Florida, 8, 23, 29

West Parish Congregational Church, 46, 106, 133

Westbrook College, 99

Western Maine Sanitarium, 104

Western Reserve, 2

Western Reserve Historical Society, 6, 134

Western Reserve National Bank, 6,

Western Reserve University, 31, 121,

Western Reserve University School of Medicine, 66, 103

Whitney, William Collins (uncle), 8

Whitney, Flora Payne (aunt), 8

Wight, I. W. (Dr.), 50

William Bingham Foundation, 138

William Bingham Gymnasium, 120

William Bingham Research Fund, 56

William Bingham 2nd Trust for Charity, 74, 126, 128, 130

Williston, Samuel, 33,

Wilson, Harry (Dr.), 100-101

Wilson, Woodrow, 36

Winsor, Robert, 43

Winter Park, Florida, 33, 109

Woodland Cemetery, 45

World War I, 28, 47, 50-52, 66, 70, 102, 125

World War II, 73, 77, 81, 98, 111, 117

Yale, 4-5, 62, 69, 81, 137

Young, Elmer, 35

Young, Philip B., 44